Introduction

Welcome to the Micro SaaS Handbook!

If you're reading this book it's likely you're in the same situation I was in several years ago - working as a 9-5 software developer but dreaming of something better. More freedom, fewer meetings, no office politics, less chaos and no technical debt to pay back etc etc.

Thankfully, I followed that nagging voice in my head and I was able to build my Micro SaaS apps up from a side-hustle to over $10k MRR, earning multiple 6 figures in subscription income which enabled me to quit my (well paid) day job and support our family of 4 👨‍👩‍👧‍👦

Eventually, I sold and exited my apps and now I'm passionate about helping other software developers like you realise you can become a Micro SaaS startup founder with your existing skills 🤓

Having experienced the full journey from idea to exit, I feel like I'm in a great position to share the wins/fails/learnings with you. So, I hope you get value from this book but please bear in mind it's just an overview of the end to end process.

If you really want to get results and stop procrastinating/over-analysing then you might want to consider applying to work with me via my coaching programme.

I've already helped several Micro SaaS founders choose their micro-niches, get lased focused on their value proposition and launch their successful MVPs and start to scale up their customer base. You can find more details on my website at https://rickblyth.com

Finally, please bear in mind that there is no such thing as failure, only welcome feedback. You're unlikely to hit a home run on your first swing. Don't give up. Keep swinging for the fences and one day it'll happen 👣

Enjoy the book!

Table of Contents

What is Micro SaaS? — 4
   Micro SaaS vs SaaS — 5
   Examples of Micro SaaS Apps — 7
      Web Apps — 7
      Browser Extensions — 8
      Platform Specific Ecosystem App Stores — 9
      Desktop Apps — 11
   My Micro SaaS Success — 11

Benefits of Micro SaaS — 13
   #1 - Compounding Results from Your Efforts — 14
   #2 - Financial Security From A Predictable Recurring Income — 16
   #3 - Minimal Startup Costs — 17
   #4 - Direct Connection With Your Users — 18
   #5 - Build It Once, Sell To Many — 19
   #6 - Time Freedom — 20
   #7 - Location Freedom — 21
   #8 - Technical Freedom — 22
   #9 - Financial Freedom — 23
   #10 - Entirely Self-Owned Business — 24
   Final Thoughts — 25

Challenges Of Micro SaaS — 26
   Final Thoughts — 31

Finding a Solid Micro SaaS Niche — 32
   Expanding not contracting — 34
   Your Micro SaaS Niche should have users with a budget for tools — 35
   Are you capable of understanding the Micro SaaS niche? — 36
   B2B or B2C or B2M? — 37
      B2B vs B2C User Characteristics — 38
   You should like your potential users — 39
   Specific and focussed — 40

Characteristics of a Solid Micro SaaS App Idea — 42
   Your Micro SaaS App Idea Must Fix a Problem — 42
      Don't Create A Solution That's Looking For A Problem — 42
      Founder Problem Fixes — 43
      Fixing a problem your customers have — 45
   It's within your (attainable) skillset — 46
   The Problem Should be Evergreen — 47
   Build your Micro Saas App on strong foundations — 48
   Final Thoughts — 49

How to Generate Great Micro SaaS Ideas — 50
- Types of Problems That Suit Micro SaaS Apps — 51
- Finding Specific Problems — 52
- Thinking Of Possible Solutions — 54
- Scoring Your Problems & Solutions — 55
- Can I Just Start Coding Already? — 55
- Final Thoughts — 56

How to Validate Your Micro SaaS App Idea — 57
- Soft Validation Checks — 57
    - Using Online Communities For Idea Validation — 58
    - Review Existing Solutions — 59
- Validate your Micro SaaS app idea by dipping your toes in — 60
    - The Dummy Order Page — 61
    - Alternative Methods To Validate Your Micro SaaS App Idea — 61
- Building the MVP — 62
- Beta testing your MVP — 64
    - How Many Beta Testers Do I Need? — 64
- Final Thoughts — 66

How to launch and promote a Micro SaaS app — 67
- Don't Delay Your Micro SaaS App Launch — 67
- Commit To Writing X Blog Articles Per Month — 68
- Gather Reviews — 69
- Build Up The Pre-Launch Hype — 70
- Houston, We Have Lift Off 🚀 — 72
- Treat Your Early Adopters Well — 72
- Start As You Mean To Go On — 74
- Failure Minimisation — 74
- Final Thoughts — 74

Preparing Your Micro SaaS App For Scaling — 77
- Customer Satisfaction Is Key — 78
- Set Goals And Celebrate Milestones — 79
- What Are Your Micro SaaS Financial Objectives — 80
- Is The App Ready To Scale? — 81
- Is The Business Ready To Scale? — 83
- Does the Pricing Model Scale? — 83
    - My Scale Fail — 84
- Final Thoughts — 85

Growing Your Micro SaaS App — 86
- Ramp Up Organic Traffic — 86
- Recruiting Affiliates For Your Micro SaaS app — 87
    - What Should I Offer to Affiliates? — 88
- Harvesting Blog Traffic — 89
- Referral Program — 90

Dropbox	90
Paypal	91
Airtable	92
Baking In Virality	93
Discoverable By Nature	95
Ramp Up Paid Traffic	95
The Traffic Campfire	96
Final Thoughts	98
How to sell your Micro SaaS app and exit	100
Why Exit & Sell Your Micro SaaS?	101
Additional Reasons You Might Sell Your Micro SaaS App:	102
Why I Sold My Micro SaaS Apps	103
Valuing A Micro SaaS Business	104
Factors Affecting The Valuation Multiplier	105
Key SaaS Metrics	105
Revenue Streams	105
Profit Margin	106
Age Of The Business	106
Niche/Market Trends	106
Business Growth Trends	106
Owner Involvement & Transferability	106
Misc Factors	107
SaaS Metrics To Constantly Monitor & Improve	107
How I Sold My Micro SaaS Apps In 5 hours (at full asking price)	108
Achieving A Top 5% Valuation Multiplier For My SaaS Business	108
Sell Your Micro SaaS App On Empire Flippers	109
Selling my Micro SaaS within 5 hours	110
Why Did It Sell So Quickly?	110
Final Thoughts	111
My Conclusions On Micro SaaS	112
My Journey From Idea To Exit	112
What's Next For Me In Micro SaaS	117
The Future Of Micro SaaS	118
How To Kickstart Your Micro SaaS Journey	119

Chapter 1

WHAT IS MICRO SAAS?

Micro SaaS apps are subscription-based applications that solve a specific problem for a niche audience. Built by a solo founder or micro-team without external funding, results compound over time in the form of a growing and predictable monthly recurring income.

Micro SaaS comes in many forms but it's the subscription-based business model that's at its core. Customers will pay a monthly/annual subscription for any software if it brings them enough value, regardless of its form.

There are great opportunities in the smaller niche markets for Micro SaaS apps to operate in which are too small for the big SaaS companies to care about.

In some cases, it'll be cloud-based software, but other Micro SaaS apps examples include desktop apps, mobile apps, browser extensions and ecosystem add-ons/plugins.

Micro SaaS apps are the best thing software developers can develop to create "passive income". Sadly there isn't anything such a thing as 100%

passive income. However, Micro SaaS is the closest thing for software developers due to its build-it-once, sell-it-to-many model. With this, your return on time invested is leveraged many times over.

Most other software development opportunities such as freelancing or permanent employment are build-it-once, get paid once and as such your income is limited by the time you can spend working.

Additionally, Micro SaaS gives you a predictable recurring income as opposed to freelancing where you effectively start from zero each month and if you don't work for whatever reason (sickness, family emergency, can't find clients etc), you don't get paid.

Micro SaaS vs SaaS

There are a number of key differences between Micro SaaS and its big brother SaaS (Software as a Service), namely:

- **Team size** - Micro SaaS apps are usually created by a single founder or run by a small micro team whereas large SaaS apps require multiple teams working across the business.
- **Investment** - Micro SaaS apps are typically self-funded, bootstrapped startups whereas SaaS apps require seed investment and then several rounds of investment raising.
- **Growth Targets** - SaaS apps have external investors bearing aggressive growth targets with the business under constant pressure. Micro SaaS startups are lifestyle businesses that can grow as per the appetite of the founder.
- **Target Audience** - SaaS businesses usually target wide audiences with a large total addressable market, whereas Micro SaaS startups focus on serving a niche audience in a very narrow and focussed manner.
- **Freedom** - Micro SaaS founders have more freedom to work when and where they want whereas SaaS owners will usually require office space and more traditional office hours across all the teams in the company.

There's nothing to stop a successfully bootstrapped Micro SaaS ramping up into a self-funded medium size SaaS or even all the way to a big SaaS company.

For example, ConvertKit was started by solo founder Nathan Barry in 2013 and spent a few years as a one man business, before first expanding out to a micro-team and eventually a large SaaS operation with multiple teams and $20 million per year!

You can even leverage the power of Micro SaaS to quit your job. In my case, I was able to start my Micro SaaS app as a side hustle and eventually after I scaled it up I was able to quit my crappy 9-5 job and live a life of Micro SaaS freedom!

Examples of Micro SaaS Apps

Gone are the days when SaaS apps were cloud-based software systems.

Nowadays, if you have a group of customers in a particular niche that pay you a monthly or annual subscription for your software regardless of its form, I'd class that as Micro SaaS.

Sure, the term Micro SaaS isn't a perfect fit, but it's a lot more succinct than "Subscription-based software for a niche group of users".

While there is an argument for SBNS (Subscription Based Niche Software), in my opinion Micro SaaS conveys the idea just fine. Here I must give a shout out to Tyler Tringas who I believe originally coined this term.

With that in mind, here's my list of the different types of Micro SaaS apps:

Web Apps

This is the staple of Micro SaaS apps and one where the customers simply access the app via their web browser. Being web-based is advantageous in that there is generally no need for the user to install the app to their local system.

Server-side, the developer can integrate with various APIs, read/write to a database, and has total control to be able to develop anything they want. That could vary from a single page application to a huge multi-module application.

Browser Extensions

This is where I've personally had success and have some experience in the trenches.

What's really unique and powerful about browser extensions is that you can enhance any website by using HTML/CSS & Javascript.

Sure, you might not build the next Honey (which sold for $4B!) but you could build something extremely useful for a specific niche that will love you for it. This is what I did, building up my own chrome extensions to the point where I was able to quit my day job.

The market size for these apps is huge, so you need to make sure you're solving a specific problem or targeting a specific niche. If not, you'll get lost in the noise of all the rest of the extensions on the chrome store and find it difficult to target potential customers.

Final note on browser extensions - as a result of a browser extension API standardization initiative created by the W3C community in 2015, you can port your extension/add-on between the major browsers without needing to majorly re-write your app.

That means your app is able to run (with some minor tweaks) on these following platforms:

- Chrome Extensions
- Firefox Add Ons
- Safari Web Extensions
- Microsoft Edge extensions
- Opera Extensions
- Brave Extensions

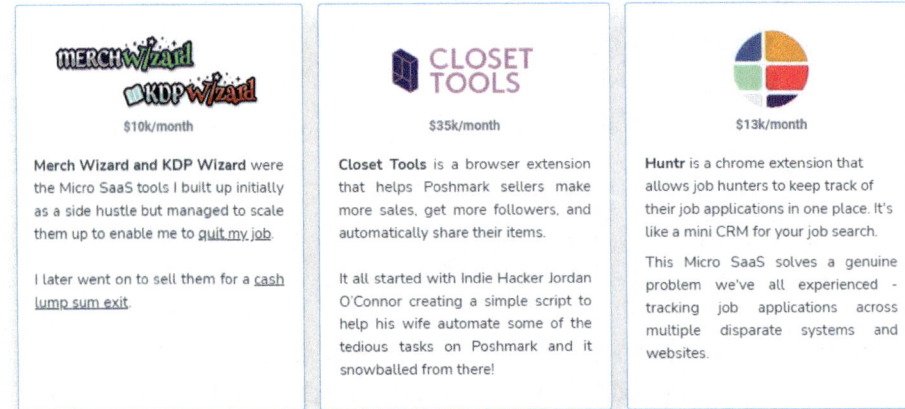

Platform Specific Ecosystem App Stores

These ecosystems are becoming increasingly popular and make it easy to build a Micro SaaS app that enhances the core platform.

This is a prime example of Micro SaaS apps piggy-backing off a successful SaaS app. It's a win-win for the core software platform as it mobilises an army of developers to fill in any gaps that the core platform has and thus help to retain their customers on their platform.

Prospective users can discover your app by searching on the platform's app store for keywords related to the problem they're looking to solve.

Another benefit is that payments are quite often handled by the ecosystem platform itself and as such are relatively friction free.

There are many app stores/plugin marketplaces online already and more on their way. Here are just a few of them:

- Atlassian Marketplace
- Intercom App Store
- Salesforce AppExchange
- Shopify App Store
- Slack App Store
- Quikbooks App Store
- WooCommerce Plugin Store

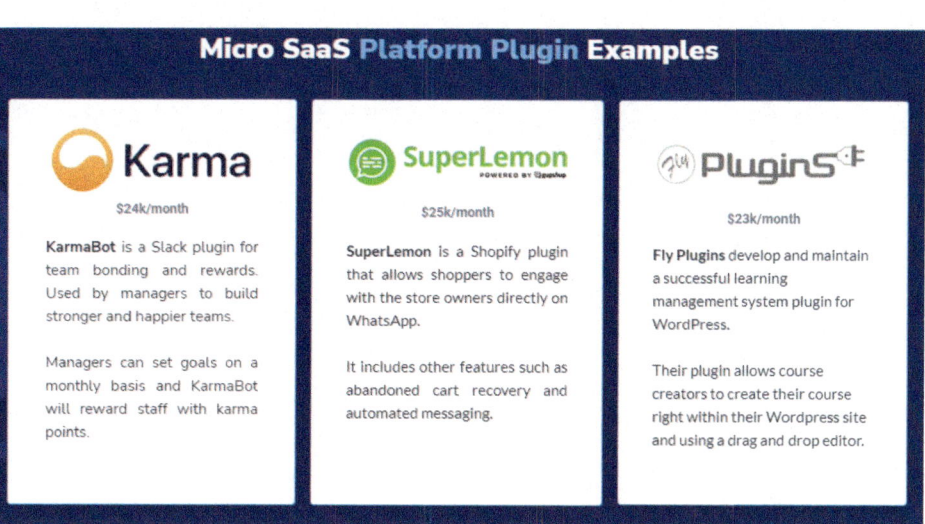

Desktop Apps

Installed on the users' computer and run locally, desktop apps can utilise native controls, are more responsive than web apps, and can be built to run entirely offline.

On the flipside, desktop apps are a little harder to update than web apps and have more challenges when it comes to trying to support a variety of operating systems and hardware.

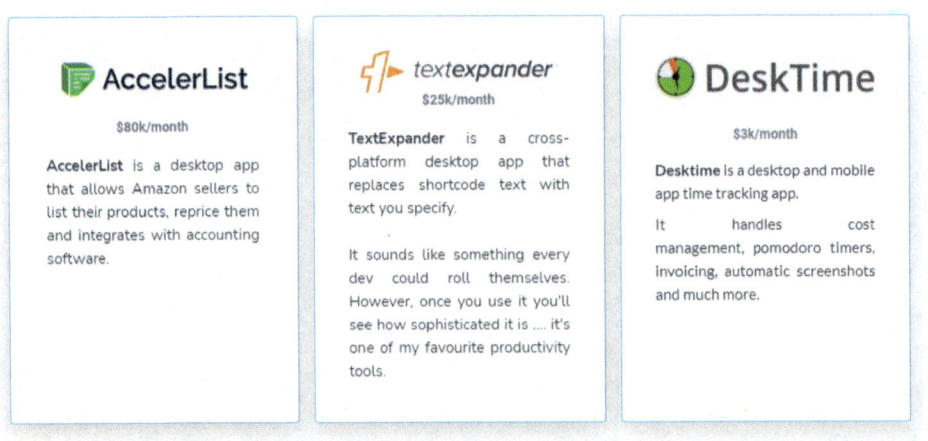

My Micro SaaS Success

In my case, my Micro SaaS apps have been my chrome extensions. Since I launched them, they have earnt me an average $10k monthly recurring revenue (MRR) which enabled me to quit my full-time job as a software developer several years ago.

After a few years of scaling my apps, I sold them for a life changing lump sum cash payment. Since then, I've made it my mission to help unfulfilled software developers around the globe escape the 9-5 through Micro SaaS.

It became clear to me that there isn't a step-by-step practical guide out there to help software developers to get started in Micro SaaS. Whether it's just starting a profitable side hustle or building a liferaft so they can eventually jump ship and quit their job to become their own Micro SaaS boss.

Having undertaken the journey of building my apps up to the point that I could quit the day job, then scaling and selling them, I feel I'm in a great position to share my knowledge with software developers around the world.

Chapter 2

Benefits of Micro SaaS

Now that we know what Micro SaaS is, let's take a look at the key benefits of the Micro SaaS business model!

At its core, Micro SaaS is about solving problems for an audience within a specific niche. Much like SaaS (Software as a Service), it allows customers to subscribe monthly/annually to software applications that add value.

So, as a software developer, what are the Micro SaaS benefits that we can expect from this business pursuit? In this article, I'll be breaking down the top 10 Micro Saas benefits, exploring the main advantages to producing Micro SaaS apps.

From minimal startup costs to financial freedom, you can expect to see a whole host of advantages. I'll be focusing on these 10 Micro SaaS benefits:

1. Compounding results from your efforts
2. Financial security from a predictable recurring income
3. Minimal startup costs
4. Direct connection with your users
5. Ability to build it once but sell it to many
6. Time freedom
7. Location freedom
8. Technical freedom
9. Financial freedom
10. Self-employed status

#1 - Compounding Results from Your Efforts

Firstly, as you add more features to your Micro SaaS app, you're building upon its existing foundations. **Instead of starting from scratch each month, you're always building on top of the work you've done in the previous month**. The more features you add, the more enticing your offering will be for your prospective users.

Secondly, your customer base will grow over time as early adopters of your app are joined by new customers. Again, the work you put in on promoting your app doesn't start from scratch each month, it compounds and builds upon what you've done previously. I cover the various methods of scaling up your customer base in a later chapter but for the time being, I just want to communicate this compounding of the subscribers too.

This compounding of both the growing features of the app and the expanding customer base cannot be underestimated.

In my case, when I first launched the MVP of my Merch Wizard chrome extension, I did so with a barebones app that was functional but didn't have any bells and whistles to it. However, the functionality in that first version laid the foundations for the app as it is today and many of the original MVP features haven't needed to be updated since their launch.

They say that you should cringe when you think about the first version of the app you release. I am cringing right now thinking about that MVP version, but you've got to start somewhere and gaining that early feedback is vital!

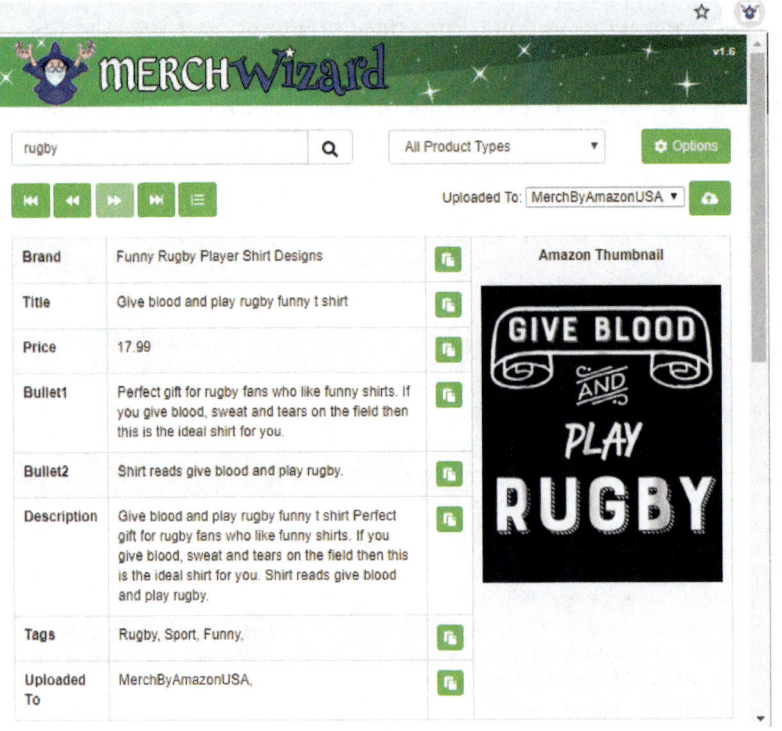

Merch Wizard MVP (Cringe)

I offered a low monthly subscription for early adopters that many of them are still paying today! This group of early adopters formed a stable base of monthly subscription income which I was able to build upon as the app evolved and became more well known within the community.

#2 - Financial Security From A Predictable Recurring Income

Your customers will subscribe to your product on a monthly or annual basis. Whilst there's always going to be a certain degree of customer churn, the vast majority of your customers will continue to pay you on autopilot every single month.

It's this automatically recurring income that makes this business model so attractive to gaining a stable passive income.

Having a baseline of subscribers paying you each month, whether or not you're working flat out adding new features or taking some time off, is very reassuring.

If you compare this to freelancing, you effectively start at zero each month with no hours billed and if you don't put in the hours, you don't get paid …. Sick? Injured? Family emergency? You don't get paid.

In my case, it was the group of enthusiastic early adopters paying monthly that gave me the confidence to focus on the app. This built up a runway to de-risk my eventual exit from my day job to go full time on the app. I wouldn't have had anything like the same level of confidence to quit my job if I was leaving to go freelancing.

I have also been through the unfortunate experience of working at a company that suddenly went bust overnight. Everyone lost their jobs with no notice and no pay.

So, let me ask you which is safer ... relying wholly on one company to pay your salary each month, or having hundreds/thousands of customers pay you a small subscription each month … I know which I'd pick!

#3 - Minimal Startup Costs

The Micro SaaS app business model doesn't require any upfront costs. The only thing you're putting "at risk" is your time.

As it's software you're creating, you don't need to buy any inventory upfront or rent office space. All you need is your computer and an internet connection to get started.

You don't even need an advertising budget to successfully launch your Micro SaaS app. My launches have all been via organic methods. I recommend this over ploughing money into paid ads which can be very costly if executed poorly.

#4 - Direct Connection With Your Users

There's nothing quite like having an open and direct connection with your app's users. They will let you know what features they love, what they'd like to see next, and will also spread the word about your app to other potential customers.

In my old day job as Technical Director, I was so far removed from the end users it was difficult to get any meaningful feedback from them.

In the Micro SaaS app world, it's likely you'll be interacting directly with your users every day. You'll have access to a continuous stream of useful insights into your users' thoughts and desires which will help mold your product roadmap.

In my case I took this a step further and organised an entire conference for my niche's user base! As I was active in the Merch Facebook groups I saw that there was only one conference for this niche, held annually in Seattle, USA.

I figured it could be a good idea to arrange a conference for the European based Merch creators and once I had the blessing from the USA contingent, the Merch UK Conference was born.

Me speaking at the Merch UK Conference

Despite the stress of organising a conference for 80+ people, which in the end had several attendees from USA & Europe as well as the UK., the benefits far outweighed the stress.

I was able to:

- Increase my profile in the community.
- Earn further trust that my app was run by a credible person.
- Create relationships with multiple Facebook group owners and network with other app owners.
- Meet many Merch Wizard users and pick their brains in person (these relationships have lasted years and are vital for feedback).

#5 - Build It Once, Sell To Many

There are only so many hours in a day and in a job/freelance role, your income is constrained by the amount of hours you're able to work. This is known as active income, where you're actively working and getting paid the corresponding amount for each hour you work. Your earning potential is always going to be constrained by the number of hours in the day/month.

Contrast that with building your Micro SaaS app. You are no longer being paid per hour, but rather for the result of your efforts in building a top notch product.

This is the secret to how you can achieve a disproportionate income from the time you invest. For example, this relatively modest looking chrome extension is **run by one developer and it nets him a disproportionate $32,000 in monthly passive income recurring revenue!**

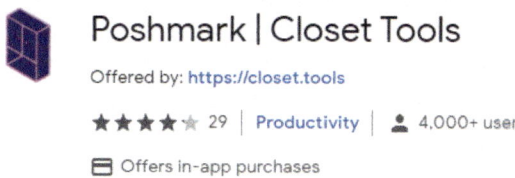

Micro SaaS apps are the best time leveraged model for us software developers to follow to achieve passive income. This leveraging of your time is the true power of the Micro SaaS business model.

#6 - Time Freedom

You develop new features and release them at your own pace. If you prefer to work in the afternoons/evenings that's up to you. **Working on your Micro SaaS app is asynchronous work.**

You no longer need to clock in and out as you do for a traditional 9-5 job. This refreshing lifestyle change opens up all sorts of flexibilities and a freedom that you don't get when you're part of the herd adhering to the corporate 9-5 agenda.

For example, I like to get out and ride my mountain bike for a few hours each week. When I was working in my full time job, the only chance I'd have would be at the weekend. The trails were always super busy and if it was raining then I'd have to get wet, as that's the only slot I'd have to go out and ride.

Now, if the weather is good on a weekday morning, I can head for the hills and ride the quiet trails with a smile on my face - it makes such a difference!

#7 - Location Freedom

As long as you have an internet connection, you can work on your app from anywhere in the world. This opens up all sorts of nomadic possibilities for those wanting to travel and work at the same time.

In my case, this came in handy when I flew over to Australia for a few weeks for my brother's wedding. I was still able to work just as effectively as I would have done at home.

In fact, whilst I was there I did several Facebook/YouTube Lives with influencers and affiliates promoting Merch Wizard from our holiday rental in Sydney. This is one of the best Micro SaaS benefits as it's incredibly freeing!

#8 - Technical Freedom

It's your choice as to whether you want to build your app in a programming language/platform new to your experience as part of your self-development or just use one that you know well to get your app to market quicker.

As you're building a new app there won't be any old creaky legacy systems riddled with technical debt to deal with. It's very likely you'll be starting with a blank canvas.

For my chrome extensions, I was able to choose between learning a new framework such as Vue/React or sticking with Angular which is what I knew at the time. Ultimately, I decided to stick with Angular for speed of delivery.

That said, for future projects, I could choose to implement them in new frameworks or programming languages as part of my own self-development goals. Technical flexibility is a huge part of the micro SaaS benefits. At the end of the day, it's up to you!

#9 - Financial Freedom

If you're an employee and you want to increase your income, your only option is to **work really hard** in the hope that your exceptional performance is noticed by management to give yourself a chance of getting a "decent" pay rise.

However, we've all had that sinking feeling in the stomach when your pay review is *disappointing* to say the least. All those hours of hard work at evenings and weekends for that tiny increase?!?

Contrast that with running your own Micro SaaS app with it's recurring passive income business model that puts you in charge of your own income.

If you want to increase your income, then you need to work on new features, keep customers happy, do more promotion, and then you'll be able to harvest the results of your additional efforts. You'll see your income grow as a byproduct of the increased level of work you put in.

#10 - Entirely Self-Owned Business

Your Micro SaaS app is likely to be bootstrapped (self-funded), with no outside investors. Worst case, you may have borrowed some money from family/friends to get the first version out the door.

As it's an entirely self-owned startup, you won't have investors breathing down your neck with ambitious growth targets. That means you'll never be working in a stressful boom or bust scenario. **You can go at the pace that is right for you.**

It's completely up to you whether you want to do it all on your own, or form a small micro-team. It's up to you how you promote the app; whether you offer seasonal discounted sales; how you work with affiliates in your niche; how you use social media; how you handle support etc…

You're the boss now.

Final Thoughts

From time and location freedom to a fresh sense of independence, there is a lot to gain by developing Micro SaaS applications. For me personally, I've been able to:

- **Earn** multiple 6 figures in subscription income.
- **Quit** my life-sapping 9-5 job.
- Banish **pointless meetings, office politics, chaos & firefighting.**
- Work **when** I want.
- Work **wherever** and in whatever **technologies** I want.
- Spend **more time with family**.
- Have a **better connection with the users** of the apps I develop.
- Have way more **financial stability**
- **Earn** multiple 6 figures when I finally exited and sold my Micro SaaS apps.

That said, unfortunately, Micro SaaS is not all rainbows and unicorns. There are some Challenges of Micro SaaS you need to be aware of before you get stuck into it. If you know what the challenges are, you'll be more prepared to overcome them when they come around.

Chapter 3

Challenges Of Micro SaaS

Although there are many benefits of Micro SaaS, this business model is not without its unique drawbacks which you need to be mindful of when starting out. Here are some of the main challenges of Micro SaaS you'll want to be aware of:

- Reliance On Systems & Platforms
- Personal Motivation Dependent
- Endless Customer Support
- Copycat Micro SaaS apps

Let's jump into the details on each of these challenges and find out how best to mitigate them.

Reliance On Systems & Platforms

If your Micro SaaS app has a heavy reliance on other systems/platforms (and their popularity/success), then you need to take this into consideration when evaluating your app idea.

For example, if you're building a plugin for JIRA, then the success of your plugin will be intrinsically linked to that of the host ecosystem. If JIRA loses popularity, you're going to be swimming against the tide trying to increase your plugin's customer base whilst the total addressable market size is shrinking.

Similarly, if you do develop a great plugin, there's always a chance that the host ecosystem might just make that functionality part of its core offering to attract more users, thus eliminating the need for your plugin overnight!

This is exactly what happened to an Abandoned Cart plugin on Shopify when Shopify decided that they wanted to make Abandoned Cart notifications a core feature of the platform 😳

This must be one of the most frustrating challenges of Micro SaaS through plugins, you can literally watch the value of your plugin disappear due to a new platform feature.

The Buck Stops With You

When you are a full time employee, you simply have to turn up to get paid. If you spend the afternoon checking out some new javascript frameworks it's probably not going to be a big deal.

However, when it's just you, if you spend an afternoon distracted by new technologies or news/social media then you're not going to have moved the needle in the right direction at all.

That said, you'll find that your mindset will have shifted from "getting through the day", to maximising what you can achieve in every minute of every day. This is because **your app is your baby** and you will want to nurture it and grow it into a successful and sustainable app.

Finally, there's no manager to escalate issues to. You have to formulate the strategy, make the tough calls and carry out the implementation.

Bring in your A-game every day if you want to make this a success.

The Hamster Wheel Of Support

To minimise customer churn, you're going to need to stay on top of customer support. If you don't respond to them in a timely manner, they'll be less inclined to share their positive experiences of the app in reviews and to other potential users in that niche.

Even worse, if they can't get your app up and running you can bet they're going to be cancelling their subscription and asking for a refund too.

My advice would be to do all the support yourself in the early days and try to get the users on a call/screenshare rather than going back and forth over several days via support tickets.

Luckily, this challenge of Micro SaaS is one that you can prevent by taking action.

I recommend having a helpdesk ticketing solution to keep track of requests. Also, where appropriate, jumping on a call with your users will save you both a tonne of time rather than going back and forth over email/tickets over the course of several days.

Plus, it's a great opportunity to ask the users for their honest feedback on the app and to hit them up for any feature requests/ideas they might have. **Direct feedback from your users is invaluable.**

Eventually, you'll invest your time into building a knowledgebase and you can also train up a support team to handle most queries. That said, be sure to make the most of the opportunity to directly connect with your users in the early days.

Potential for Copycats

If people within your niche see your app gaining popularity, they may look into launching a competing product. In certain cases, they blatantly rip off the features of your app and sprinkle some UI changes on to make it appear different.

To minimize copycats and their effects you'll want to ensure any client side code is obfuscated and try to perform as much of the app's magic server side where possible. In some cases, this just isn't possible and you have to go into it with your eyes wide open.

The best way to combat copycats is to offer the best in class customer experience, listen to user feedback, implement feature requests and continue to innovate and introduce new features to keep your app's offering more appealing than any potential competitors.

Final Thoughts

While there are a great deal of personal and professional benefits to the Micro SaaS business model, you shouldn't ignore the challenges either.

In the trying moments, try and remember why you're following this path. Take a second to remember all the benefits of developing Micro SaaS apps. After all, it's not all doom and gloom!

Alright, enough negativity already …

Let's look at how to get started with Micro SaaS, the first step being how to find a great target niche for your Micro SaaS app.

Chapter 4

Finding a Solid Micro SaaS Niche

As the saying goes, **the Riches are in the Niches**. Finding a great micro niche is a fundamental part of Micro SaaS; otherwise it'd just be plain old SaaS with a wide audience.

Instead of looking for huge markets with few identifying characteristics, you want to niche down to a micro-niche that has a highly targetable potential customer base for your app. For example, think about how you'd go about targeting the following user base:

- *Case Management Software*
- *Case Management Software For Professionals*
- *Case Management Software For Lawyers*
- *Case Management Software For Real Estate Lawyers*

BROAD ⬇ MICRO

The more micro you go, the better. Not only will you be able to find and engage with potential customers much more easily, but you'll be able to serve them better with a much more tailored solution.

Imagine being a Real Estate Lawyer and searching for a Case Management Solution …. you'd immediately be drawn to the below link as it is so specific to you:

> https://www.practicepanther.com › blog › legal-case-ma...
> **Legal Case Management Software for Real Estate Lawyers**
> 17 Aug 2016 — Legal **Case Management Software for Real Estate Lawyers** · One of the best features of a · such as PracticePanther is the flexibility in regards to ...

As opposed to the generic offering below:

> https://www.hoowla.com
> **Hoowla: Case Management Software**
> Modernising legal **case management software**. Well known for it's conveyancing software we covers all areas of law. Find out why so many law firms choose ...

With that in mind, the next step is to find a few micro SaaS niches that could be a good fit for you. You're not yet looking at the possible problems/solutions in these niches, rather just shortlisting a number of suitable niches you're interested in exploring further.

Here are some of the key characteristics you'll want to look for:

- An Expanding Niche
- A User Base With Budget For Tools
- An Understanding Of The Niche
- A B2B, B2C, or B2M Niche
- A Specific and Focused Niche
- A Customer Base That You Like

Expanding not contracting

Clearly, we don't want to be building apps for a niche that is in decline. Instead, we want to be targeting niches that are either stable or ideally expected to grow (hopefully significantly) over the next 5 to 10 years.

If it's an emerging market, there will be less competition and you may be able to claim a stake of the market early on. You have to balance that approach against the "safer", more established niches that have been and will be around forever (accountancy, law, health, etc).

The first Micro SaaS apps I developed were chrome extensions for Merch By Amazon creators which certainly was (and still is) an emerging niche. I came across this niche whilst looking at passive income opportunities myself.

The Merch niche is mainly made up of graphic designers & entrepreneurs, uploading their art to Amazon to sell on various apparel products. Each time Amazon sells a product with their design on it, they're paid a small royalty. This platform and niche only started in 2015 but it has expanded exponentially since then.

Whilst Amazon doesn't release the actual number of creators on the platform it was fairly easy to estimate the size of the community by looking at the size of Facebook groups, Reddit channels etc.

Critically, I could see that the community was increasing week by week, with more members joining the groups all the time. Merch was a great niche to get into as it was certainly up and coming, plus the creators made money each time their designs would sell. All I needed to do was to create some apps that would allow the creators to focus on what they really wanted to do - create more bestselling designs.

Take a look at this Google Trends graph below showing how this niche has grown in popularity and whereabouts in the growth phase I launched my apps and finally when I was able to quit my day job!

Your Micro SaaS Niche should have users with a budget for tools

What does your typical user look like? Are they a business or a consumer? Do they have a budget to spend on your solution?

For example, if they're students, you're going to struggle to convince them to spend what little money they have on a monthly subscription to your study-system app (ahead of video games and beer).

Conversely, let's say you have built a great Shopify plugin that automates emailing potential users when a product is back in stock. If your plugin only takes 5 product sales a month to justify the cost of your plugin, it's a clear win-win value proposition for all concerned (just be mindful that one day Shopify could potentially re-create your plugins' functionality within its core offering making your app redundant 😱).

Do the users in the niche spend money on tools right now? If it's already the case, then this is certainly comforting. If not and you're attempting to be the first, then you better have a damn good value proposition for your end user.

This should take the form of how much time or money your app can save or make them - which will be a no-brainer for the user.

Are you capable of understanding the Micro SaaS niche?

Ideally, you're already passionate about the industry/niche and are already knowledgeable in this sector. Maybe you're thinking of solving a common problem that you've seen from your day job or from freelance work.

If not, then you should consider how long it would take you to get up to speed with the niche's users. For example, whilst the Health & Fitness niche is relatively easy to relate to and understand, trying to understand hedge fund derivatives trading is going to be far more challenging.

That said, if you can compete in these complex (and lucrative) sectors, it can certainly give you an advantage.

B2B or B2C or B2M?

An important consideration is the type of users your user base would contain. For example, it could be:

- **Business to Business (B2B)** where your customers are other businesses. Examples from Micro SaaS up to SaaS include UpVoty, Plutio, Slingshot, Salesforce, Atlassian & Hubspot.
- **Business to Consumers (B2C)** where your customers are consumers. For example, Nomad List, Canva & Duolingo.
- **Business to Many (B2M)** where your users are a mixture of businesses and consumers, for example there's my app KDP Wizard which has a mixed user base of publishing businesses and also entrepreneurial consumers selling low-content books on Amazon. In big SaaS, there's Dropbox which has enterprise offerings as well as personal plans

There are significant differences in what you're getting yourself into when targeting a B2B niche vs a B2C niche. The main one being in the sales cycle:

- **B2B** requires an outbound sales team to call out to target businesses. Usually there are lengthy sales, legal & contractual negotiations per business to convince multiple people to give the green light. Whilst the recurring fees are much larger than B2C, the cost of acquiring a new customer is significantly higher than that of B2C.
- **B2C** is almost always self-service sign up with lower recurring fees and a short sales cycle as there is usually just one person making the purchasing decision. Costs of acquisition are much lower than B2B as most of the time there is no outbound sales team in B2C.

B2B vs B2C User Characteristics

It's also worth considering where the users for your niche gather as you'll want to build up a presence on these platforms if you haven't already got one.

B2B users are likely to spend their time on LinkedIn & Twitter. Whereas, B2C users can be found on social networking platforms such as Facebook/Instagram/Reddit/Twitter etc.

Churn is typically higher in B2C than in B2B due as the consumers haven't jumped through all the hoops that would have been jumped through during a B2B sale. Consumers are also more unpredictable than a business, as they let their personal bank cards breach limits or don't update the card details when they expire and simply drop off the radar.

Conversely, with a B2B solution, there's a contractual agreement and the business will continue to pay the subscription whilst the solution is working for them and there's still a need for it within the business.

Depending on how you feel about the above (setting up a sales team vs income vs churn vs targeting) will dictate which niches are a good fit for you.

You should like your potential users

Would you be ok hanging out with your prospective users?

You will certainly be regularly connecting with your users in the future, whether it's at conferences (in-person or virtual), webinars, seminars, screenshares, Facebook groups, emails, support calls, support tickets, etc.

If the thought of spending time talking to a niches' user base makes you shudder, then you're setting yourself up for a tough road ahead. Whether it's due to them being extremely demanding or dull or whatever … you're best to steer clear if possible.

In my case, the Merch user base is mainly made up of graphic designers, side hustlers, entrepreneurs. These users are fairly laid back and love any tools that help accelerate the growth of their Merch business.

When I had been in the niche for a while, I noticed that there was only one annual conference for this niche, held in Seattle, USA. For some reason, I thought it would be a good idea for me to arrange a conference for the UK/European based Merch creators, even though I'd never organised a conference before!

Hosting this conference for over 80 people was quite stressful, and in the end it turned into a much bigger event than anticipated with several attendees flying in from USA & Europe, as well as the UK.

However, I was able to meet many of the users in the niche, build relationships, establish trust, and crucially pick their brains in person. Many of the users that came were already Merch Wizard users and getting their feedback and ideas for new features made all the effort worthwhile.

Specific and focussed

Instead of building for a generic market that's hard to target, it's going to be much easier to target a specific set of people.

I like to compare it to fishing in a small, undiscovered pond that not many other fishermen know about. This small pond only has one species of fish in it and you become an expert on that fish, knowing exactly what type of bait that fish loves. Contrast that with casting your fishing net far and wide into the ocean and trawling for hours to try to catch as many fish as possible, even if some of those fish aren't what you're looking for.

If we relate this back to the earlier case management example, you'll struggle to target leads given that a broad number of niches could use such an app. How would you find out where your potential user base hangs out? Would your generic solution resonate with them? Probably not.

It's far easier to immerse yourself into a community of Real Estate Lawyers and see if you can solve their PITA problems with your app idea.

Now we've got a handle on the characteristics of the niche/market we're aiming for, let's look at **the characteristics of the proposed app itself.**

Chapter 5

Characteristics of a Solid Micro SaaS App Idea

By now, hopefully you've selected a target niche and you're looking at possible app ideas for that niche. Let's dive into some of the characteristics of a great Micro SaaS app idea.

We'll be covering the following attributes of a solid micro SaaS app idea:

- Fixes A Painful Problem
- Not A Solution Looking For A Problem
- Has An Attainable Solution
- The Problem It Fixes Is Evergreen
- Built On Strong Foundations

Let's take a look at these in more detail.

Your Micro SaaS App Idea Must Fix a Problem

Whilst it is possible to create something that improves people's lives, you'll have far more interest in your app if **it is actually fixing a painful problem** that the users are experiencing. These problems need to be genuine problems that are in dire need of a solution, rather than temporary irritations.

Don't Create A Solution That's Looking For A Problem

Always start with the problem, rather than the solution. Whilst it's tempting to create something that just popped into your mind, it's likely that you'll fall head over heels in love with the idea and simply have your blinkers on.

You'll tell yourself that it's a wonderful idea, maybe even "the one!". In reality, when you start with a solution in mind rather than a problem in mind, it's likely you'll find it difficult to attract an audience seeing as nobody is searching for a fix for a non-existent problem. You'll be wasting your time trying to convince people that they need it in their lives.

Building a Micro SaaS app without focussing on a specific problem for a targeted audience will vastly reduce your chances of success. **This is one of the big issues for products that launch on Product Hunt - many of these apps are solutions in search of a problem and launch in search of a user base that may or may not exist.**

Self-Operating Napkin

An example of a solution searching for a problem

Founder Problem Fixes

The majority of Micro SaaS apps are created to overcome a problem that the founder is experiencing themselves.

This was true in my case too. I created my first app when I was trying to upload designs using the Merch By Amazon UI.

At the time, you could only edit one product at a time, there was no way to open another product in a new tab. Being constrained to one tab like this felt like a full-on violation to my rights as a modern day user of the internet 😂. I also saw others complaining about this on the Merch forums and Facebook groups.

Problem identified!

Within a weekend, I'd created my first chrome extension - Merch Batch Editor. It was a super simple and incredibly ugly chrome extension, but users responded really well to it. I set a one-off price of $12.99 for this app. But, even with the low price, I had very low expectations that anyone would want to buy it. After all, I wasn't going to run any ads to it, just rely on organic traffic methods.

However, I was soon proved wrong as this super-basic tool made me over **$3,000**!

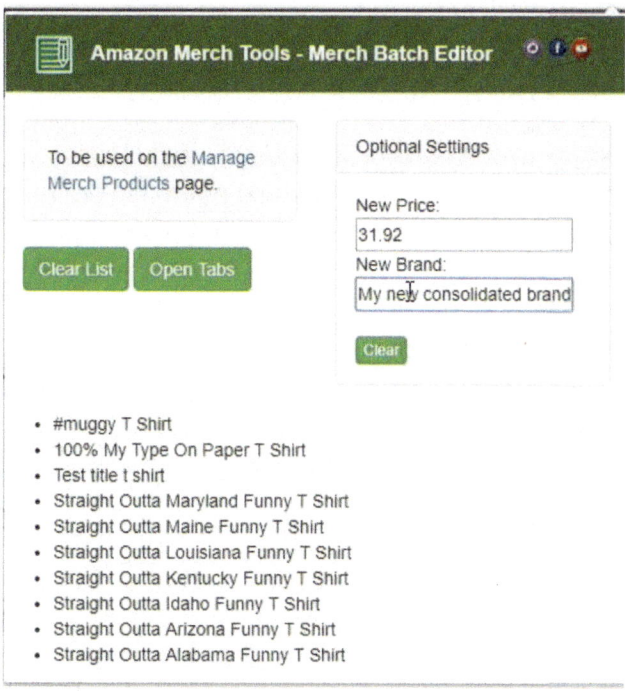

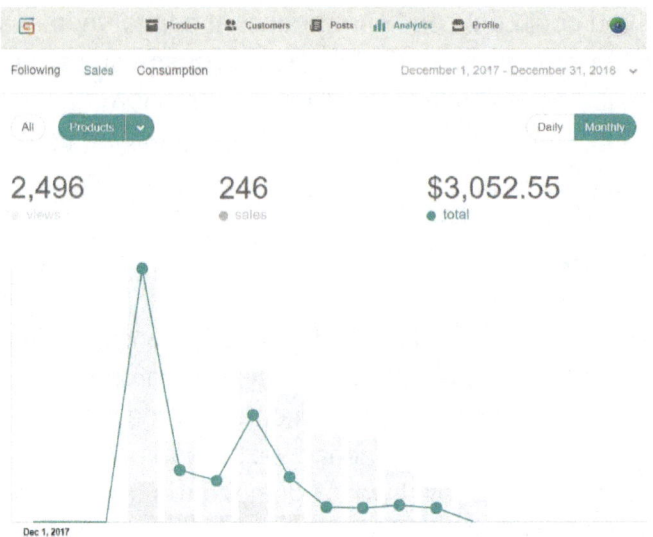

The butt ugly Merch Batch Editor …my first chrome extension which took a weekend to develop but made me over $3k

This small app was the building block to my bigger chrome extensions and helped me earn the trust of the users and build a reputation in the community as a trustworthy app developer.

Fixing a problem your customers have

Another reason to create a Micro SaaS app is to fix a problem your clients/customers are experiencing. It could be that in your full-time job or freelance work you see a recurring problem for which there isn't a viable solution yet.

Is there a way you could create something that plugs in the gap?

Just remember though, if you don't like the industry/clients you service in your day job/freelance work, then it may not be the best fit for you.

For me, when I was working in my full-time job as Technical Director of an Insurance Software business, I could see plenty of gaps in the market for some Micro SaaS apps.

But, the problem was that after 10 years of working in that same industry, I couldn't think of anything worse than building more software for insurance brokers 🥱

It's within your (attainable) skillset

Is your app idea something that you can build with your current skillset? If not, you'll need to factor in how much time you need to allocate to training up in the required technologies before you can even start building your app.

Building an app in the Augmented Reality space would be super cool. But, if you're going to burn all your energy/time just getting to the start line, it's a non-starter.

Also, bear in mind that if you plan on using new technologies to create your first app, it's likely that your app is not going to follow best practice for those technologies.

After all, you'll likely be gluing together code from tutorials and fixes from StackOverflow just to get the thing up and running. It'll take some time before you're capable of creating apps in these technologies using the best possible practices.

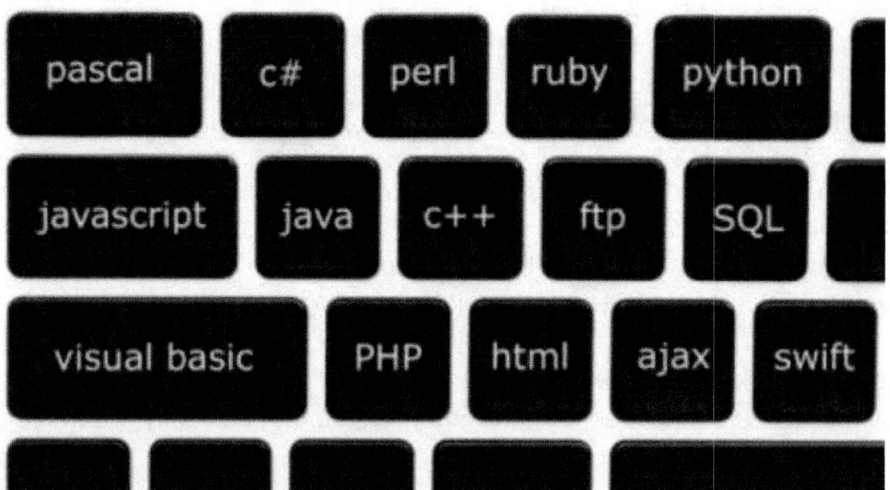

In my case, my 20 years of server-side coding skills (ASP .Net, C#, SQL Server) didn't help me much when it came to developing my first chrome extension using Javascript/CSS/HTML.

However, these skills were fairly easily attainable, and within a few months, I was up to speed. That said, it still took a year or two to really get into the best practices for developing chrome extensions.

The Problem Should be Evergreen

Can you imagine people searching for possible solutions on Google/YouTube for this problem year-round? If not, then it's unlikely you'll have a steady stream of potential customers finding your app's website.

The problem you're solving should be a long-term, constant pain for your user base. You don't want to fix a problem that is seasonal or only going to be around for a short period of time.

There is one exception to this rule though. This is when you're creating a quick app to fix a short term problem so you can gain trust in the community and obtain leads for your longer-term app idea.

This is what happened with my first app, Merch Batch Editor, which I mentioned earlier. It fixed a short term problem that was only around for about 12 months.

It only took a weekend to throw together and whilst it made me $3,000, more importantly, it gave me 250+ emails of highly targeted niche users that proved they're happy to buy tools that help them fix their problems.

During the launch of my next app in this niche, I was able to email all of these people with a discounted offer and kickstart my app's user base.

Build your Micro Saas App on strong foundations

In an ideal world, your app should stand alone without relying on other systems and businesses. At least, you'll want to minimise your dependency on other businesses. I'm not saying don't integrate with anybody else's APIs, just be mindful of the foundations that you're building your app on.

For example, if you're building a custom Shopify app, then you have a strong reliance on Shopify continuing to grow its customer base so you have a steady stream of potential new customers.

In Shopify's case, you'll probably be fine but imagine if you went all-in on building an app for SnapChat only to see your user base heading for the doors in their droves due to a SnapChat UI update!

You need to map out all the systems your app will rely on and look at the level of risk associated with each one. Then, create a contingency plan for what you'd do if one of them went out of business.

For example, my chrome extensions have a strong reliance on Airtable to store the users' data (in their own private Airtable bases). In the unlikely event that Airtable went bust, I had a backup plan to swap out Airtable for

Google Sheets instead. It wouldn't be quite as powerful as Airtable, but it would certainly work as a backup.

Final Thoughts

As you can see above, it's critical that your app isn't just simply some software that you fancy building. Instead, it really must revolve around fixing a painful problem that a niche group of users are experiencing and will likely still be experiencing for the foreseeable future.

Finally, you'll need to consider the foundations you're building your app on and from a technical perspective, whether it's within your attainable skillset.

Next, let's get on to the exciting step of actually **generating great Micro SaaS ideas**.

Chapter 6

How to Generate Great Micro SaaS Ideas

The best Micro SaaS ideas solve specific problems for a specific niche user group. These problems will likely be costing the target users time and/or money.

Therefore, the key to generating solid Micro SaaS ideas revolves around simply being able to identify these problems and come up with a solution that fixes them.

Your users should be able to see your app as a no-brainer solution in terms of the value it brings vs the cost of the subscription.

In this article, I'll cover the following topics so you know how to come up with great Micro SaaS ideas:

- Types of Problems That Suit Micro SaaS Apps
- Questions To Ask Yourself
- Finding Specific Problems
- Thinking Of Possible Solutions
- Scoring Your Problems & Solutions
- Micro SaaS Idea Examples & Case Studies

Types of Problems That Suit Micro SaaS Apps

Micro SaaS apps are great at fixing many common "problem" scenarios, for example:

- Automating repetitive and/or tedious tasks.
- Performing calculations that are currently calculated manually.
- Connecting disparate systems.
- Replacing Excel spreadsheet workarounds.
- Plugging in gaps of missing functionality in host ecosystems
- Enhancing reporting
- Etc.

Bear these scenarios in mind when you go searching for problems. Ask yourself:

- How could software help with this?
- Could I automate this tedious process?
- Is it possible to surface more data to improve the user's experience?
- Could I make this easier/less painful?

- Would I be able to create an app that streamlines this lengthy multi-step manual process?
- How could I provide an integration between these systems?

Finding Specific Problems

You'll want to compile a list of problems that you could fix. Don't pass judgment on these as you add them, instead just focus on listing them out.

The majority of Micro SaaS ideas form apps that are designed to overcome a problem that you (as the founder) are experiencing. It makes sense that if you're experiencing this pain then it's likely that others are too.

List out all the problems or even just inefficiencies that you're frustrated with now - focus on tedious things to do or actions you wish were less time consuming.

The second most popular reason to create a Micro SaaS app is to fix a problem that your clients/customers are experiencing. It could be that in your full-time job or freelance work you see a common problem for which there isn't a viable solution yet.

Add them to your list of identified problems which we'll use later on to figure out which problems are genuinely worth fixing.

The third way to find problems is to research the issues the potential users of your previously identified niche/market are complaining about.

How do you find these problems? By finding where your target users hang out and joining their community spaces. These communities could be in the form of forums, Facebook Groups, Subreddits, Slacks, Discords, etc. Immerse yourselves in these communities, and you'll see certain complaints cropping up repeatedly. Add these to your list of potential problems to solve.

Also, don't be afraid to post asking users if they could wave a magic wand and fix a problem in that niche's domain, what would it be?

Another way to generate Micro SaaS ideas is to ask about your friends & family and see if they're frustrated with any of the sites/software they use.

A great example of this is the Closet Tools chrome extension, created by Jordan O'Connor to help his wife automate some of the tedious tasks on Poshmark.

It started off life as just a simple script, just to help out his wife with some mundane tasks on Poshmark. He'd shared this script within the community and received great feedback, so much so that he made it into a chrome extension and the rest is history!

What started off as a script to solve his wife's problem, evolved into a great Micro SaaS product that fixed a common problem Poshmark sellers experienced, which in turn **led him to scale his app up to $32k MRR as a solo founder!**

Closet Tools on IndieHackers.com

Thinking Of Possible Solutions

Once you've completed your list of problems, the next thing to do is to go through the list and figure out what the high level solution would look like to solve each of the problems.

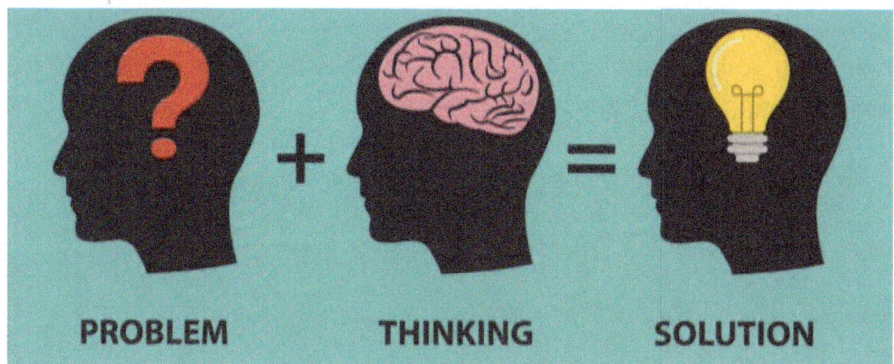

Is it a web app that would fix this problem? Maybe it's a desktop automation app or maybe even a chrome extension? Think about all the possible tools that could be used to form a great solution for the user.

Ask yourself, is it something you could build yourself (or with a micro team) in a reasonable timeframe? Is the solution within your (attainable) skillset? If not, then strike it off the list.

Rinse and repeat until you have a list of viable solutions for the problems you've previously listed.

Scoring Your Problems & Solutions

Now you'll have a completed list containing your identified niches, their problems, and high level app ideas that are within your attainable skillset. You're now ready to work through your list of Micro SaaS ideas and pass judgment!

Work through your list and score each opportunity based on the niche, the problem and the proposed solution.

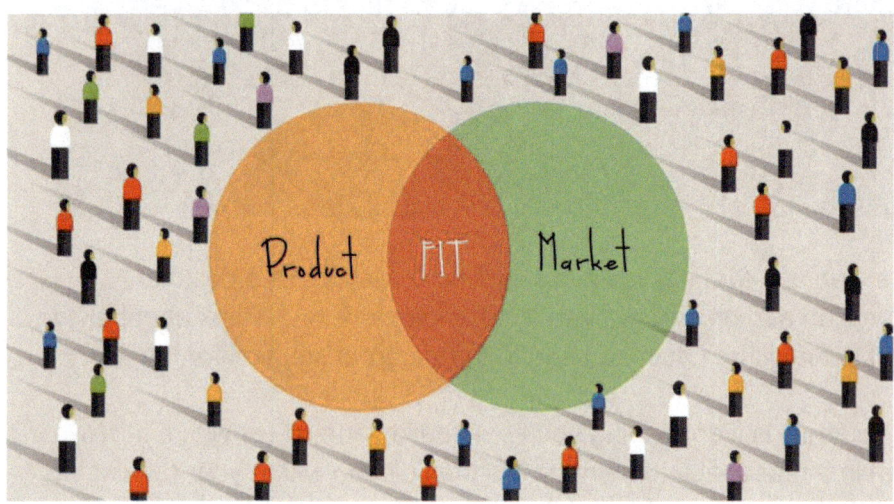

Can I Just Start Coding Already?

In short, no. Please don't take the top scoring app idea and start coding (with your head buried deep in the sand) for the next 6 months. No matter how "certain" you are that it'd be a hit, you're likely to be setting yourself up for a delayed failure.

I suggest taking your time to pick your top 3 app ideas and then mulling them over even more.

As you revisit them each day, you'll have different thoughts, feelings, and perspectives on them. These could lead to finding yourself falling in or out of love with the ideas as you go.

It's better to get these mixed feelings out in the open before you start building anything.

Final Thoughts

Whilst it's tempting to open up Google and search for "micro saas ideas", nobody is going to give you an exclusive idea for you to develop and monetise. At best, you'll be able to find some inspiration or jumping off points to start from.

The key to coming up with Micro SaaS ideas is to find genuine, evergreen, PITA problems that a niche's users are experiencing. Get all these listed out and evaluate what you can do to solve these problems for them.

At this point, you should have a variety of potential app ideas to consider and you'll want to pick your favourite(s) for validation.

Next, let's take a look at how you can validate your Micro SaaS idea ...

Chapter 7

How to Validate Your Micro SaaS App Idea

Whilst it's possible to do some soft validation techniques, there's really only one way to fully validate your Micro SaaS idea - build a barebones MVP (Minimum Viable Product) version of your app, put it out there and see if people will pay for it.

But before you start building the MVP, you can also utilise some soft validation checks before you go ahead and code your app:

- Soft Validation Checks
- Using Online Communities For Idea Validation
- Review Existing Solutions
- Dipping Your Toes In
- The Dummy Order Page
- Alternative Methods To Validate Your Micro SaaS App Idea

We'll then move on to look at how to build your MVP and how to beta test your MVP.

Soft Validation Checks

Revisit and re-validate the niche & problem with a fresh set of eyes, how many people are in your target niche, is it evergreen, and are they searching for a solution to this problem? Here are a few ways to look for search intent to get a feeling for the numbers.

- **Google Trends** - Check the popularity of your target niche. We want stable/growing rather than declining.

- **Google Keyword Planner** - Find out approximate search volumes for software in your target niche. Add your specific problem search term to this if it's common enough.

- **Keywords Everywhere chrome extension** - (*a great example of a Micro SaaS app idea itself*) - Repeat the above to give some further indicators of search volume.

- **UberSuggest** and **AnswerThePublic** - Gain more insights and to spark further ideas.

Using Online Communities For Idea Validation

Next, move on to the places online where your niche's users hang out in communities. This could be Facebook Groups, Reddit subs, Slack, Discord, etc.

Join these communities and use the search function on the platform to find people's thoughts on the problem you're considering fixing and the workarounds. If possible, try to message these people one on one in a non-spammy way and if appropriate, outline your high-level app idea to them to get their feedback.

Be wary that it's easier for them to give **you a false positive by encouraging you to build it**, so make a point of asking for honest feedback and how much they'd pay for that solution.

Review Existing Solutions

Next, check out any existing solutions to the problem. If there aren't any solutions or there are only manual workarounds, then you may think you've struck gold and that your solution must be better than no solution right?

Well, there may be a good reason why others have passed up on the opportunity, so make sure you do your due diligence and consider all angles carefully.

If there are already some solutions in place for the problem it doesn't mean that they've got it 100% right and it's a non-starter for you. Look for the gaps or issues users have with the existing solutions:

- **Are they too expensive for the users to justify?** Could you produce something more affordable? For example, Pabbly is a slimmed-down, cheaper version of Zapier and it is becoming very popular proving there's plenty of room in the market for both of these platforms to thrive.
- **Are they bundled with too many other features?** Start your app off with just one core module that provides an express service.
- **Are they hard to understand or use?** Build something that is easier to set up and use.
- **Are they missing key features?** Build these as your USP key starting features.

Validate your Micro SaaS app idea by dipping your toes in

Are you happy with what you see and you are ready to take your idea to the next level? You can then gauge demand and receive feedback before committing to building an MVP by creating mockups of how the app would look and function.

It should be obvious to the end-user what the app's features would be from a glance at these mockups.

You can then share the mockups via private messages with contacts in the niche or even post it publicly in the niche's communities and ask for their honest feedback. Be wary of prying eyes when posting publicly. If you have many users screaming "take my money already" in the comments, it's possible that somebody in that niche could hire a developer to build the app.

I'd suggest removing the post after a day or two once you've gotten the feedback you're looking for. That way, it'll reduce the chances of someone stealing your Micro SaaS app idea.

The Dummy Order Page

You can take this a step further and build a simple website for the app with the above mockups in it along with some short paragraphs outlining the key features. This technique was made famous by Tim Ferris's "4 hour workweek" book.

You'll have buttons on the site encouraging the visitor to order the app. On the "Order" page it's up to you whether you:

1. Simply state that the app is in development and prompt the user to join the waitlist to receive a discounted launch offer.
2. Frame it as an app that's available to order/pre-order and you actually pretend to take their card payment to truly validate how many people will actually pay for the app. Of course, no payment is taken and the user is told as much.

You can then drive traffic to the site through paid ads and check the clickthrough rate to "order" and, if nothing else, gather prospective users' emails ahead of your genuine launch.

Alternative Methods To Validate Your Micro SaaS App Idea

Personally, I've not needed to create an app website as above to try to gauge demand ahead of a launch as I could see the demand right in front of my eyes.

For my target niche, Merch By Amazon, I was already part of the community. I listened to many Podcasts and watched lots of YouTube videos on the subject in my spare time.

Within the Facebook groups and on these Influencers' shows, I was able to spot recurring problems within the niche which plenty of people were complaining about. This alone gave me enough confidence that it would be worth building at least an MVP version of an app that solved them.

Instead of building out a website with a dummy order/pre-order page, I actually started by offering some simple free chrome extensions. The users only had to register their email address to gain access to them.

This helped to build up trust in the community and to gather an email list of leads within the niche that were ripe for targeting when I was ready to launch my main app.

Building the MVP

The MVP is our proof of concept and will find out the answers to these key questions:

- Does this app solve a real problem for a real set of users?
- Are those users willing to pay for this solution?
- Is it possible to target and attract users?

The majority of us software developers are somewhat perfectionists. You have to throw that out of the door for your MVP, or risk losing weeks/months of your life for no good reason.

You have to move quickly, fail fast … fail forward.

The first version of the app should be basic, have lots of missing features and potentially be a little rough around the edges. But, critically, it has to function correctly.

First impressions count and we're aiming for a reaction like *"woohoo, someone is starting to fix my problem, how can I support them to improve their app so it works better for me"*, rather than, *"this app looks like a 5-year-old designed it and it's full of bugs"*.

Throwaway or Foundational MVP?

In my view you have two options when creating your MVP:

1) Hack it together to such an extent it does a job and proves if there's a demand for the product. Throw it away and start again if your MVP gets traction.

2) Spend more time on your MVP with the intent of forming the foundations on which you're going to build the final app upon.

In some cases, you'll even be able to use no-code solutions to quickly knock up a functional MVP.

No-code tools such as Bubble.io are becoming increasingly powerful and are great if your app is a web/mobile/desktop app. However, you will struggle to go down the no-code route if your app is a chrome extension or ecosystem plugin.

Beta testing your MVP

Before we actually launch the MVP, ideally we're going to want to get some feedback from users within the niche to help mold the MVP into shape before its public release.

Assuming that you have no ready-made audience to tap into, you'll want to dive into your niche's communities and find some beta testers to help give you valuable feedback on your MVP.

Find recent posts where people are complaining about the problem your app proposes to fix. Either comment on this post or message the users privately, letting them know you're creating an app to help fix this problem.

Let them know you're going to be launching a beta version of your Micro SaaS app idea in X weeks and you're looking for people to give feedback on it over a period of X weeks. In exchange, you can either offer them a big discount off the launch price or even free lifetime access if you have to.

How Many Beta Testers Do I Need?

You need 5-10 beta testers to get some decent initial feedback. Put them into a group (Facebook group/Slack workspace) so they can see each other's feedback. This will ensure they're not duplicating each other's issues and suggestions.

Structure and streamline the feedback loop to make it super simple for them to give feedback. After all, their feedback will be as precious as gold to you.

Quick reality check - as with all things, some beta testers will never open the app and will just drop off the radar. That's why you ideally need a bunch of them to actually get some valuable feedback.

Ok, you're getting closer to having a functional and bug-free MVP version ready to roll that our beta testers are happy with. It's likely that your beta group will be bombarding you with feature requests and it'd be worth putting together a quick high level feature roadmap which you can then use on your website to show potential users how your app is going to evolve.

Final Thoughts

Validating your idea is critical to ensure you don't waste your time building a product that nobody wants. In this article, I've outlined the high level idea validation process which is:

- Soft Validation Checks
- Using Online Communities For Idea Validation
- Review Existing Solutions
- Dipping Your Toes In
- The Dummy Order Page
- Alternative Methods To Validate Your Micro SaaS App Idea
- Building An MVP
- Beta Testing your MVP

Exit criteria for this phase is a group of Beta testers that are "happy" that your app is functioning correctly and a provisional roadmap of planned features.

At this point, we're getting close to the most exciting and nerve-wracking phase of this journey - the launch phase! Let's take a look at how to launch and promote your Micro SaaS app.

Chapter 8

How to Launch and Promote a Micro SaaS app

At least 30-60 days out from your Micro Saas app launch, you'll want to start to build up an audience to launch to. Alongside this, you'll need to be planning out your launch channels.

But that's far from everything. You should be actively trying to do the following things when getting ready for the exciting day:

- Don't Delay Your Launch
- Commit To Writing X Blog Articles Per Month
- Gather Reviews From Beta Users
- Build Up The Pre-Launch Hype
- Launch Your Micro SaaS!
- Treat Your Early Adopters Well
- Start As You Mean To Go On

Let's take a look at these in more detail. I've also included an in-depth guide and review of my own 5-figure Micro Saas app launch that you can download completely for free!

Don't Delay Your Micro SaaS App Launch

So, you've (hopefully) kicked your MVP (Minimum Viable Product) into shape, and it's ready to make its debut. **Please resist the never-ending temptation to "add just one more feature before I launch"**. We all know that once that feature has been built, there'll be another one, then another one 🔄

You don't want to fall into the trap of going round in circles adding new features, constantly delaying the launch for one more week or even months at a time.

Commit To Writing X Blog Articles Per Month

When in the pre-launch phase and you're still building out your website, it's easy to forget to focus on other content.

It may seem like devoting time to writing blog articles isn't worth it at this stage. However, these search engine-friendly posts will give you a great long-term ROI, so it's worth planting these seeds nice and early. With better Google Rankings comes more traffic, with more people finding your website due to the well-written blog posts.

With that in mind, commit to writing a number of blog posts that you'll publish per month. This could be anything from one a month up to several each week to get the blog bulked out at the start. The main thing is to commit to a regular schedule so that you don't end up with an outdated-looking blog.

It's important to attract an audience and keep your audience engaged with relevant content. Make sure your articles are well crafted and give value to your target audience. These articles will provide you with a steady stream of (free) leads for your app every single month. You can also use these blog posts as lead magnets so potential users can opt-in to your email list.

Articles should answer questions around the problem that your app solves. You should also aim to cover the full spectrum of intent from informational through to commercial and transactional intent.

- What is Case Management Software ?
- What are the benefits of Case Management Software?

INFORMATIONAL

- Best Case Management Software For Lawyers
- Case Management Software For Lawyers Reviews

COMMERCIAL

- Buy Case Management Software For Lawyers
- Subscribe to Case Management Software For Lawyers

TRANSACTIONAL

You might think you need to wait until you have the app ready to launch before announcing it to the world but as long as you're ready with your marketing efforts, you can start showing people what you're going to offer well before you launch your app.

Gather Reviews

If you've been through the beta testing phase, then now is the time to ask them to gather reviews which you'll put on the sales page/website as testimonials. Any social proof will really help build trust and in the early days this is essential!

Disclosing that they're a beta tester will add to the authenticity of their reviews. Get consent from them to use their profile pic/social avatar to add a further aspect of social proof to their reviews.

Below you can see some reviews of one of my Micro SaaS apps - Merch Wizard. In the early days, I had automated email sequences that culminated in a request for a review from the user.

 Merch Wizard has allowed me to add listings much faster than I could do on m own. It organizes all my listing info so I have it in one place. There are many ways to sort and group the information in the database so it can be found quicker. It's a miracle tool! One you absolutely must have in your MBA toolbox.

Veta Sue Gilbert 2 years ago

Complete Game Changer! Got me so organized. I found success with merch but was completely overwhelmed with being organized to scale my shirt designs to other products. This has got me so organized, I can find and easily access all my listings and pngs. Also helps uploading speak x100!

Cj Johnson 2 years ago

This is an incredible tool at an incredible value. It pulls together all the disparate parts of your Merch business and puts them all into the same place for easy editing, storing and relisting. Saves so much time!!

And, the tech support is awesome. I was up late trying to get an issue cleared (yeah, it was user error - me) and Emily was available to help and stuck with me while I worked through the issue.

Highly recommended!

Dave Cadoff 2 years ago

Merch Wizard Reviews

Build Up The Pre-Launch Hype

On to the actual micro SaaS app launch itself! Set a realistic date and then start to build up some excitement for the launch 🚀

Starting from T-minus 30 days, every few days you should be providing some fresh content for your potential user base. **This content shouldn't just be the "X days to go" style mundane countdown email sequence.**

Build up a content calendar in which you'll drip feed them each feature's description and the benefits of it to them. Believe it or not, people will genuinely get excited for your app launch if you're drip feeding them solutions to their problems.

Here's an example of a simple post I made in the KDP Wizard Facebook Group showing a searchable treeview control I'd been working on to replace the clunky native treeview control. Despite its simplicity, the group's users loved it because they knew it'd save them so much time every time they listed a book:

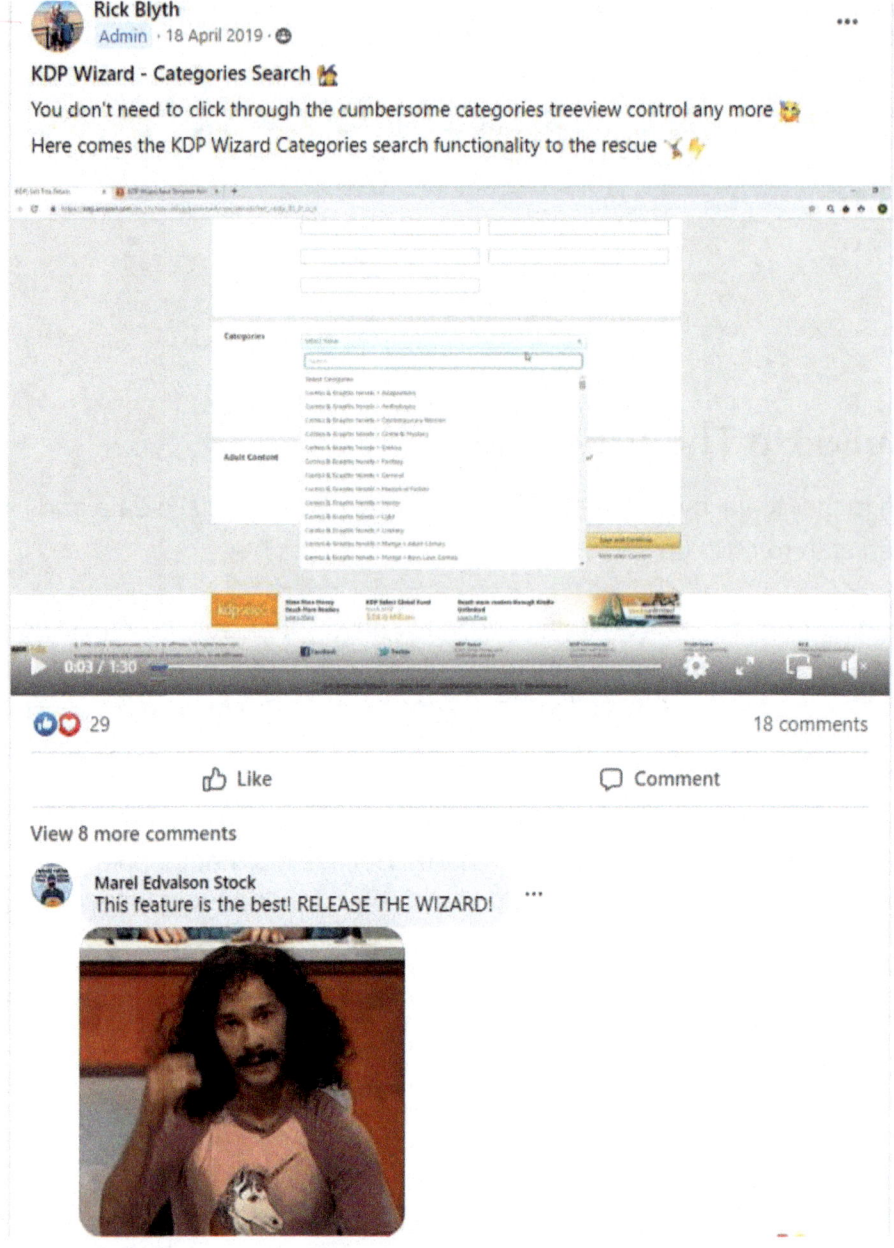

Houston, We Have Lift Off

Needless to say, your beta users should have tested the go-live version ahead of you starting to promote the app. Once they've given it the green light, it's time to push the big red button and get this Micro SaaS rocket launched.

You can start small and launch through one platform at a time to ensure there aren't any teething or unexpected load issues. As your confidence builds, you can expand out to the bigger platforms.

Some users may struggle to get your app up and running, so you will need to be on hand to help support this influx of new users.

Treat Your Early Adopters Well

Your first users will be the seeds of your customer base, so it's important you treat them well. Be transparent in your pricing, provisional roadmap, and your passion for making the best possible app to solve their problem(s).

If you can do a great job for these early customers, they will likely help spread the word of your app to other potential users in your niche. This chain reaction is only likely to come from delighted users rather than just satisfied.

The MVP of my app Merch Wizard was very "basic" (to put it kindly), but it did what it needed to do. It proved that there was an audience willing to pay for an app to fix their problem. Many of those early adopters are still paying their monthly subscription several years on as they locked in the low monthly launch rate.

Merch Wizard MVP (cringe) 😱

Start As You Mean To Go On

Even though we're just starting on our app development journey, it's important to set off on the right foot with the future in mind.

Yes, you can hack your way to an MVP and then address that technical debt later on - I'm ok with that.

However, from a billing perspective, subscribers to your MVP should be paying your **business** stripe/paypal account rather than your **personal** stripe/paypal account which would be way harder to transfer during a future sale (albeit a long long way off).

Having been through the sale/exit process, I have learnt that subscription income that can't be easily transferred can sometimes be written off the valuation. 😳

Failure Minimisation

Nobody wants their app launch to flop. If you've done your best to Validate Your Micro SaaS Idea, then you're already on the right track.

In any case, you're better off finding out the truth sooner rather than later to avoid unnecessarily wasting additional weeks/months developing a product nobody wants.

If your initial micro SaaS app launch does fail, don't be disheartened! It's most likely due to a lack of genuine demand for the solution you're aiming to provide, rather than a reflection on yourself. You can learn from this experience, finding a better problem to focus on for next time.

Final Thoughts

This has been an exciting chapter, actually launching your app into the big wide world! Let's remind ourselves of the key takeaways for this chapter before we move on:

- Don't delay your launch - you'll always want to add more features, there will never be a right time, the fear of failure etc .... ship it as soon as it's working and functional and get that early feedback!

- Commit To Writing X Blog Articles Per Month - this early time investment can provide you with a steady stream of new leads for your app on an ongoing basis.

- Gather Reviews from beta testers/early adopters - in the early days, social proof will really boost your conversion ratio as more potential customers read the benefits other similar users are experiencing.

- Build Up The Pre-Launch Hype - engage with your audience, drip feed them whatever you can, no matter how small to build up anticipation of your launch.

- Launch! - start small and build it out as your confidence grows that you're able to support the growing user base.

- Treat Your Early Adopters Well - ensure support is rapid and timely. Try to overdeliver where possible to leave early adopters with a glowing feeling about your app and the person/team behind it.

- Start As You Mean To Go On - make sure you're billing users via an appropriate payment processor that connects to your business account, not your personal account! You don't want to have to try to migrate these users later on as many might drop off. Similarly, you'll struggle to have revenue from these users taken into account during a valuation.

In order to successfully scale your app's user base, you'll need to go through a short period of consolidation to sure up the foundations first. These are important prerequisites to ensure that when you do scale your Micro SaaS, it goes smoothly.

Next, let's take a look at preparing a Micro SaaS app for scaling before you go ahead and scale up.

Chapter 9

Preparing Your Micro SaaS App For Scaling

Just like launching a real rocket, when you launched your Micro SaaS app, it would have taken a metric tonne of effort just to achieve that initial lift-off and get it a few feet off the ground. The great news is that the following stages build upon the momentum from your launch and will help propel you to outer space (or just quit your day job if that's your target!).

Before we jump into the methods to grow your Micro SaaS app, we need to run through some important prerequisites to ensure that when you do scale your Micro SaaS, it goes smoothly:

- Ensuring Customer Satisfaction Remains High
- Setting Goals And Celebrating Milestones
- Discovering Your Financial Objectives
- Is The App Ready To Scale?
- Is The Business Ready To Scale?

Let's take a look at them more closely.

Customer Satisfaction Is Key

I have put this point first on the list as it really is that crucial. **You must always have a happy user base, it will be the foundation you build upon.**

Underpromise and overdeliver; engage with your users; have a transparent roadmap and overdeliver on the features that the users are expecting.

If there are support issues, resolve them as quickly as possible - whatever it takes! I recommend screenshares where possible for an expedited resolution and in turn, happier customers.

This is even more essential in the early days as you try to:
- Build trust in the community.
- Ask existing users for reviews.
- Minimise churn (% of users cancelling their subscription).
- Encourage early adopters to refer other users (we want them to be gushing about the app).

Customer satisfaction really is the foundation of the growth process. There's no point in having a high number of users try out your app only for them to leave the next month due to it being buggy and support taking ages to come back to them.

Take this snippet from a review of my app Merch Wizard, which was left by an early adopter who was super-impressed with the rapid response of myself and the support team. Imagine being a prospective user and reading this review, you'd be reassured that even if you did have any issues running the software, they'd be resolved very swiftly.

Merch Wizard is the answer to all my "wish list" requests for an easy to use, effective, and robust software that has ALL the features I need to store, organize, edit, and upload my listings.

Additionally, the customer service is the best I have experienced in the Merch arena. Rick and his team are very responsive to Facebook messages and group comments. It doesn't seem to matter what time of day or day of week it is, I always get answers back within a couple of hours...many times within minutes. It has become an indispensable tool in my arsenal and has saved me countless hours of work with so many amazing features to store, organize and edit over 8,000 listings. If you have thousands of listings in your inventory, then you owe it to yourself to get the Merch Wizard ELITE. It is worth every penny...and then some. Thanks to the team at Merch Wizard for all you do for the Merch community. It is much appreciated!

Jay Bayne *a year ago*

Set Goals And Celebrate Milestones

Take a deep breath and look at where you were 12 months ago, or even 6 months ago, and how far you've come through the process of planning and launching your own Micro SaaS app.

Think about where you are now and where you want this to go next. It's time to set some SMART goals which are:

- **S**pecific
- **M**easurable
- **A**ttainable
- **R**elevant
- **T**imely

Your targets can be based on almost any aspect of your Micro SaaS business, for example:

- **Financial Goals** - $5,000 monthly recurring revenue within 6 months
- **User Goals** - 1,000 active subscribers within 3 months
- **Growth Goals** - 20% growth year on year
- **KPI Goals** - Less than 5% churn by December; LTV per user of $500 within one year

- **Referral Goals** - Have 5% of our new users come via referrals next quarter
- **Content Marketing Goals** - Publish 100 blog posts by Christmas
- **Social Media Goals** - 500 Tweets within 6 months; Increase Followers to 25k on Facebook by Easter

For each of the above, work backwards from where you want to get to and figure out the stepping stones on the way. These will be your milestones and should be written down along with a target date for each milestone.

Don't just write these down and shove them in a draw to be forgotten.

Instead, check-in on them regularly and correct your course where possible. That which isn't measured isn't improved upon!

When you hit a milestone, don't forget to celebrate it! Yes, there will be a new milestone to set, but you should reward yourself (and your micro-team if you have one) each time a milestone is achieved.

What Are Your Micro SaaS Financial Objectives

Ask yourself what you're hoping to achieve financially with this Micro SaaS app. Is it just some extra side hustle money (beer money), or perhaps it's your aim to be able to pay your rent/mortgage (rent money) with this additional income?

Maybe, you hate your corporate job in software development and want to build up your cash-generating Micro SaaS so it enables you to finally quit your day job!

Clearly, there's a correlation in the amount of income vs the amount of effort you need to put into your Micro SaaS app. Wherever you're heading, your specific financial target will dictate how you set about growing your user base.

If it's just beer money then you won't need to scale as aggressively. Someone that is planning on quitting their software developer job in the next 6 months to live the Micro SaaS life of freedom will have to scale harder.

Is The App Ready To Scale?

Before we try and attract boatloads of additional users, your Micro SaaS app needs to be able to handle these new additions without compromising the performance that other users currently experience. Otherwise, you'll find that a similar number of users that are coming through the front door are leaving through the back door!

If your app is server-based, then there are tools you can use to simulate a large number of users. As a minimum, you'll want to ensure that all three of the below tests pass with flying colors:

- **Load Testing** - simulate high loads, check that the app still functions correctly

- **Stress Testing** - check recovery from extreme loads, server crashes etc.
- **Volume Testing** - bulk out your database as to what it would look like with 10x the data in it. (Did somebody say database Index)?

Side note - I am presuming that your app isn't just running on a single server and is likely cloud-based 👆 ... otherwise you don't need me to tell you twice that you will need to stop reading this article and go and re-architect the app to make it scalable.

In my situation, my apps are chrome extensions that run within (you guessed it) a user's Chrome browser. Whilst this sounds great from a scalability perspective as all of the code is client-side, it does make hundreds of calls to external servers every minute.

Fortunately for me, I don't have to administer these servers as the endpoints belong to Airtable, Amazon, and Gumroad. As such, my apps are by their nature, unconstrained and unaffected by a sudden influx of new users (lucky me!).

Is The Business Ready To Scale?

Ok, now we've established that the app can scale - but what about your Micro SaaS business?
How will customer satisfaction be maintained as the number of users increases and the volume of support tickets increase? Do you need to hire and train up a small support team?

Tip - early on, invest your time into creating a detailed knowledge base. It will pay dividends for years to come. Users can find their own solutions to issues and you can direct support tickets to the relevant articles rather than repeating yourself. On my second app, KDP Wizard, we had the knowledge base, tutorial videos, and setup videos/articles in place pre-launch (we were confident of a successful launch). We received lots of positive feedback on the smooth setup experience and the wealth of support articles available.

If you've managed to handle support so far with something primitive like email or Messenger, then **now is the time to level up to a ticketing system**. There are plenty of free/cheap helpdesk solutions nowadays and customers will expect this even from small Micro SaaS apps.

From your perspective, having the ability to assign tickets, re-use response snippets and ultimately have a searchable database of tickets will make your life easier too.

At the other end of the business, do you have the bandwidth to cope with the increased volume of pre-sales enquiries from potential customers as the app is being promoted? They will expect quick responses to any pre-sales questions. Slow responses at this stage may put them off from buying entirely.

Does the Pricing Model Scale?

It's also worth considering how your pricing model will work at scale. Are there any costs within the business that will scale disproportionately to the revenue?

One thing to be mindful of is the scenario where you offer a lifetime deal on your app but you have some associated transactional costs as the users use your app.

My Scale Fail

Scaling caught me out within my own app Merch Wizard. One of the features is the batch language translation of 5 textboxes from English to a destination language. This started off as just English to German as that was the only marketplace available with a different language (so a total of 5 API calls per Merch listing to be translated).

I used my Amazon Translate account which the chrome extension called. I absorbed the cost across the user base, simply thinking of it as a subsidised cost of running the app.

However, two factors contributed to my translation costs skyrocketing:

1) Merch introduced several new marketplaces totalling 5 destination languages. So, instead of 5 x 1 translation API calls, it rose sharply to 5 x 5 = 25 translation API calls per listing!
2) The user base increased as the app gained popularity. Not a problem normally, but as I'd sold many lifetime licences (notably to big Merch creators) during seasonal sales, each time they carried out batch translations it was eating into my profit margin.

In the end, I had to bring the free translation to an end and ask the users to sign up for a free account to individually utilise the free monthly allowance from Amazon Translate. Instead of just delivering this bad news to the user base directly, I figured it'd be a good time to add some new translation providers that they'd asked for (Google Translate and Deepl).

I was able to sell it to the user base as giving them a more configurable solution where they could pick their preferred translator. On the whole they were very happy with that!

Final Thoughts

Ahead of actually starting to scale your Micro SaaS app you've got to ask yourself the key questions discussed in this chapter, namely:

- Can I scale whilst retaining high levels of customer satisfaction?
- What are my scaling goals & milestones along the way?
- What are my financial objectives? Do you want beer money, rent money, to quit your job or big money from your Micro SaaS?
- Is The App Ready To Scale?
- Is The Business Ready To Scale?
- Does the Pricing Model Scale?

Having laid the foundations carefully, we're on to the exciting topic of actually scaling up both your user base and recurring income.

It's vital that during this growth phase that customer satisfaction remains high. You must keep on top of support, continue to add the features promised on the product roadmap. You can then look into utilising SaaS marketing techniques highlighted in the next chapter to scale and grow your Micro SaaS app.

Chapter 10

Growing Your Micro SaaS App

By now, you'll have checked off all of the items in the preparation stage. Next, we're on to the exciting topic of actually growing your Micro SaaS app user base and subscription income.

It's important that even during this growth phase, you don't lose focus on customer satisfaction. Make sure you keep up to date with support, add the features you promised on the roadmap, and then get on to attracting more users to your app through SaaS marketing.

That said, let's take a look at the key strategic elements of growing your Micro SaaS app:

- Ramp Up Organic Traffic
- Recruit Affiliates
- Harvesting Blog Traffic
- Referral Program
- Baking In Virality
- Discoverable By Nature
- Ramp Up Paid Traffic

Ramp Up Organic Traffic

Now that there's a healthy foundation of happy users for the app, it's time to start growing your Micro SaaS organically, spreading the world far and wide and finding new subscribers.

If you have built up an email list and not yet emailed all of them through your launch cycle, now is the time to email them.

If you have built up a Facebook group for your niche or if you've become an active (and contributing member) of any other groups, then now is the time to raise awareness around your app within these groups.

All my Micro SaaS apps have been marketed purely via organic traffic. Sure, it's more effort than running ads, but in the long term it'll give you a great ROI.

Recruiting Affiliates For Your Micro SaaS app

Outside of your initial launch audience, if you don't have a Facebook group or email list to market to, then the quickest way to increase your customer base will be through tapping into affiliate audiences.

In exchange for promoting your app to their audience, the affiliate will receive a percentage of the income generated through the promotion.

Initially, this may not sound appealing, and you're probably thinking it's not a fair deal. You've done so much hard work and now you're likely to have to give this person around 25%+ of the recurring income received from the promotion, just for sharing it to their audience!?!

What you might not appreciate - and initially I didn't either! - is that these affiliates have likely spent several years building up an audience that trusts them.

They will have given valuable content to their audience, engaged with them, moderated the content in the group, vetted new members etc. There's also the daily grind of moderating the group for spammers and scammers which can be a real time suck.

Having grown several Facebook groups from 0 to over 5,000 members, I can tell you first-hand that it's no small job to build an engaged community.

Bearing all that in mind, the affiliates are not going to want to push a product that they've never heard of to their precious audience without good reason. One bad promotion could seriously damage their hard-earned reputation.

Treat your affiliates well and you'll be rewarded with a long term symbiotic relationship.

You need to demonstrate to the affiliate that your app will genuinely help their audience.

What Should I Offer to Affiliates?

There are several things you can, and should, offer to your affiliates to ensure you have a good working relationship. You should offer them:

- A demo of the app and access to its features so they can try it out
- High percentage commissions that make your app worth promoting
- Regularly updated marketing collateral
- Open lines of communication they can message you quickly
- Commissions that are paid on time

Over the years, I was able to forge many great relationships with affiliates in the Merch By Amazon & Kindle communities. I went on several live shows on Facebook & YouTube reaching global audiences that I would never have reached on my own. Each time I went live, I would always do a live demo of the app (what could go wrong 😂) and take questions live.

Yes, it's not the most comfortable way to spend an hour, but it was always well worth it as they produced an influx of new subscribers paying a recurring subscription fee.

Harvesting Blog Traffic

Remember the blog posts you committed to in the Micro SaaS Launch chapter? By now, you'll have crafted a range of blog posts on a variety of targeted topics that will resonate with your target niche. **It's now time to reap the rewards and harvest the fruits of the digital seeds you've sown.**

You should have a steady stream of visitors to your site and you should now begin to steer these visitors towards becoming users of your app, either subtly or directly by creating a call to action for each article.

As a reminder, each blog article will have an associated target search intent as below:

- What is Case Management Software?
- What are the benefits of Case Management Software?

INFORMATIONAL

- Best Case Management Software For Lawyers
- Case Management Software For Lawyers Reviews

COMMERCIAL

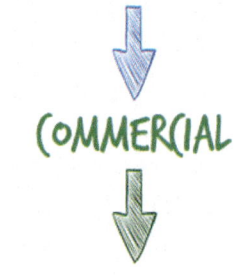

- Buy Case Management Software For Lawyers
- Subscribe to Case Management Software For Lawyers

TRANSACTIONAL

Depending on each article's topic and target search intent, you'll set up an appropriate call to action on each article. Here are some examples for you:

- **Informational Posts** - download our white paper on case management software (sent to their email).
- **Commercial Posts** - download this independent review of the top 5 case management software apps (sent to their email).
- **Transactional Posts** - get started with a free trial of our case management software (requires user account creation via email).

You'll start to build up a healthy email list of leads for your app. Depending on their entry point, you can send them an automated unobtrusive, value-driven email sequence.

Naturally, these emails will give your leads a gentle nudge that will eventually drive them towards becoming paid customers.

Referral Program

You can think of a referral program similar to the affiliate program discussed earlier. Except, in this case, it's your customers that are doing the lead generation for you rather than relying on affiliates and their audiences.

You can choose to create an ongoing referral program for a steady stream of consistent leads or create short-term referral contests with prizes to try to generate a large number of leads quickly.

Make it super easy and rewarding for each customer to earn a bonus or (worst case) cash when they refer a new paying user. Increase the chances of your referral program going viral by **offering a double-sided reward so there's a bonus for both the referrer and new customer**.

Here are some great examples of powerful SaaS referral marketing examples you can take inspiration from:

Dropbox

Quadrupling their growth within a year after introducing their referral program, Dropbox soon grew into a billion-dollar company. Their referral program was simple. For every new customer you referred, you got bonus storage space for the lifetime of your account. It started off as 500MB of storage space but if you had Dropbox Plus it was 1GB of storage space per referral which soon added up!

Get up to 16 GB of free space by inviting your friends to Dropbox!

For every friend who joins and installs Dropbox on their computer, we'll give you both 500 MB of bonus space (up to a limit of 16 GB)!
If you need even more space, upgrade your account.

Invite your friends by email

Add names or emails

Send

Paypal

With an app that revolves around money, it's only natural to offer a cash incentive in this case. Initially, PayPal gave $20 to anyone opening a PayPal account and $20 to the referrer. Later they lowered these rewards to $10 and finally to $5 per signup.

At the time of writing, Paypal is still employing referral marketing to great effect:

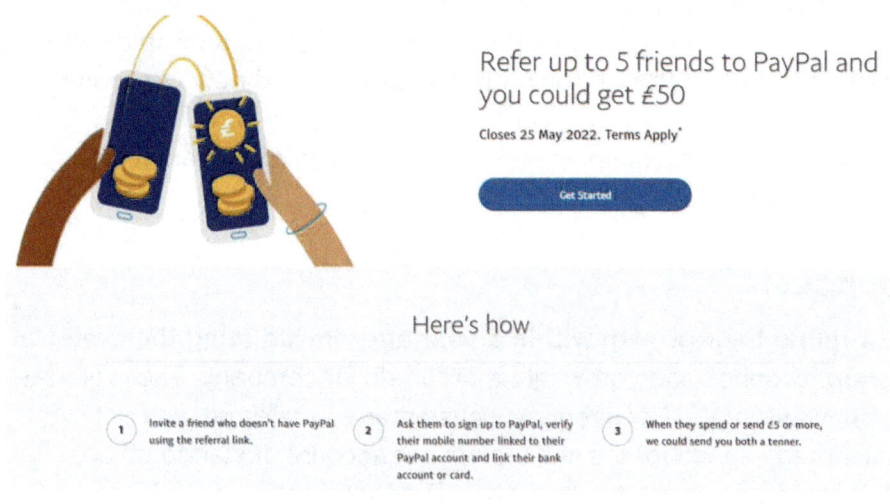

Airtable

Offering a simple but effective credit-based referral scheme, Airtable gives the referrer $10 credit for anyone that signs up using their link. The new customer doesn't even need to sign up to a paid plan or make any purchases for the referrer to be credited $10.

Creating an account takes less than 30 seconds and with no credit card required. You can literally get a year's worth of Airtable Plus just by asking your family & friends to take 30 seconds out of their day to register a free account.

As my chrome extensions rely heavily on Airtable, I have personally benefited from the Airtable referral scheme. **I baked my referral link into my apps and their setup guides and before I knew it I had over $3,000 in Airtable credit!** I've used some of this credit on a Pro workspace but most of the time I've not needed to dip into my credit as my Airtable bases are generally small enough to live on the free tier.

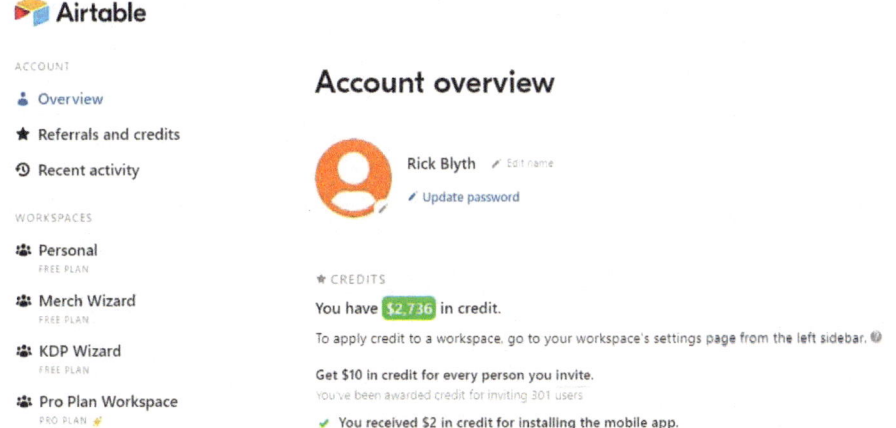

Think about what kind of referral program would make sense in your app. Would one of the below referral reward models work in your Micro SaaS app:

- Discounted subscription fee.
- Additional usage allowance.
- In-app bonuses/unlocks.

- Tier-based swag.
- Money that they can cash out (this should be the final resort).

Remember, if you can make it double-sided so both referrer/referee win, it'll vastly increase the chances that your referral marketing program will go viral.

Baking In Virality

In addition to offering incentives to share links to your app as above, consider **creating shareable moments within your Micro SaaS app**. This would usually take the form of something that the user has achieved and would be proud to share with other users within their niche.

This is best explained using an example of a chrome extension called PrettyMerch which is in the same Merch By Amazon niche as my apps. PrettyMerch shows creators their sales and royalties in a pretty graph with advanced analytics that are way beyond what's available from Amazon's native reporting pages.

As Merch is based on tiers, the app celebrates when a user "tiers up" with a popup that users love to screenshot and share to the community to celebrate their levelling up.

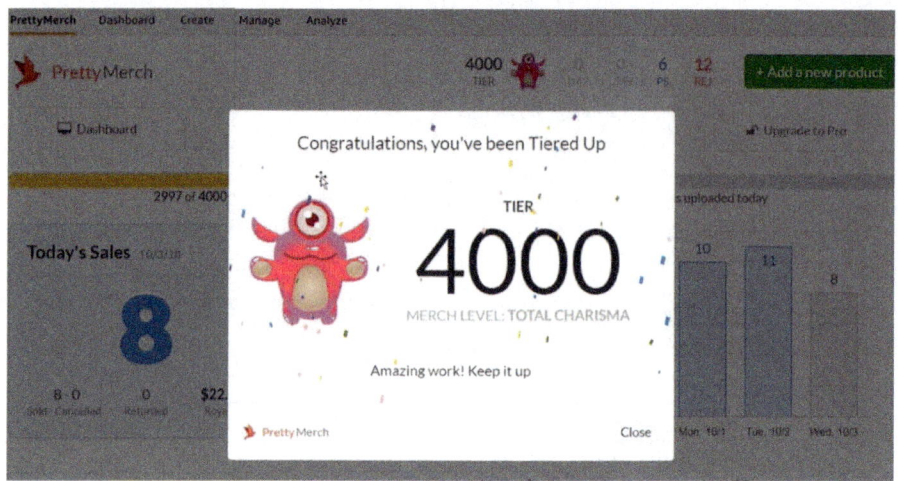

In addition to that, people are always sharing their sales numbers (they can mask out the product details in one click).

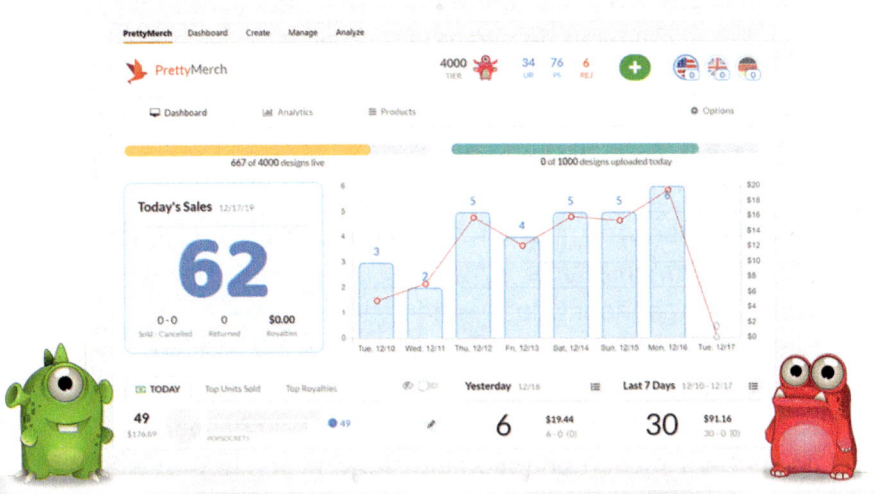

When a Merch creator sees the screenshot containing the beautiful charts and advanced analytics, they'll also notice that they can trial the app for free. Before you know it, they've installed it and are well on the way to becoming a paid subscriber!

Let's think about the cost of acquisition for each of these customers... that's right, $0! The existing customer base is just spreading the word throughout the community for free. No affiliate to pay, no referral credit to absorb.

The virality from creating these memorable and easily shareable moments are well worth the time invested in gamifying your application. Heck, there's plenty of libraries that will help with this that you can just plug into!

Discoverable By Nature

One way that you can make your app highly discoverable is through the nature of the app itself. This occurs when users share links to your app to non-users who may not even be aware of your app.

Here are some examples of large-scale and Micro SaaS apps that are intrinsically shareable and discoverable by their nature.

- **Calendly** - book a timeslot in my calendar without any need for back and forth on emails.
- **Zoom** - let's connect virtually and share screens.
- **Slack** - let's collaborate in multi-channel real-time chat.
- **Google Docs** - let's work on this online document together.
- **Dropbox** - let's back up and share large files between us.
- **Loom** - here's a screen recording showing you how to work.
- **Balsamiq** - here are some mockups of the new UI.
- **Upvoty** - here's our product roadmap and central place to manage feature requests.

Can you create an app that solves a specific problem and is by its nature shareable? If so, you'll benefit from huge organic growth as the number of users spreading the word about your app increases exponentially.

If you manage to make your app discoverable by nature, then growing your Micro SaaS app becomes a breeze.

Ramp Up Paid Traffic

Finally, whilst paid traffic seems appealing, it's best employed only after careful consideration.

There's no point in paying for a load of ads to just find out that your core offer isn't resonating with your target audience. This could be due to a number of issues such as:

- Poor product/market fit.
- Solution in need of a problem.

- Over or under pricing.
- Seasonal problem.
- Poor ad targeting.

The point being, you need to first prove that your offer converts via the above organic methods before growing your Micro SaaS app via paid advertising and accelerating the process.

The Traffic Campfire

I like to think of organic traffic vs paid traffic akin to building a campfire.

You want to set up a foundation of large slow-burning blocks of wood (your organic content marketing/referral marketing/affiliates etc). This will ensure that the fire will burn steadily for a long period of time. You will consistently add to these foundations over time (more blog articles/referral schemes/affiliate partnerships).

Once the fire is burning well, you can pour on some gasoline (paid advertising) to increase the height of the fire for a short period of time.

However, gasoline can be expensive and is also out of your control. The price of gasoline (cost of ads) can skyrocket and ad accounts are notorious for being shut down (leaving you with zero traffic) so you can't rely on this alone.

Instead, over time, you'll use a blend of both organic and paid traffic sources. This will mean you'll enjoy a steady stream of new leads coming into your world, along with more short-lived focused advertising campaigns.

Whilst this could be a whole article on its own, I'd recommend starting your paid advertising with YouTube Ads and Facebook Ads. They're both great platforms to place ads and once you have a winning ad, you can scale that out to a wider audience and increase your customer base accordingly.

Final Thoughts

Growing your customer base is a great and rewarding phase of the Micro SaaS journey. Let's just remind ourselves that each month, we don't start at zero. We have a steady income stream and now we want to carefully split our time between growing the user base and delivering a kickass product.

Let's recap some of the key points from this chapter before we move on:

- **Organic Traffic** - continue raising awareness of the app through your own channels - Emails, Facebook Groups, Twitter, etc.
- **Affiliates** - they have the audience, you have the product. Keep your affiliates happy and they will be very rewarding for you.
- **Harvest Blog Traffic** - continue to pump out the blog content and harvest the fruits of the digital seeds you've sown.
- **Referral Program** - spend some time figuring out what makes sense for referral rewards in your app. If you can motivate your existing users to refer others you'll be well on the road to success for sure!
- **Bake In Virality** - what shareable moments can you create in your app? Does gamification make sense in your app?
- **Discoverable By Nature** - this isn't always possible but if it is, then you want to make it easy for non-users to see the value in your app and to check out an account for themselves.
- **Paid Traffic** - this should only be considered when you know you have a proven offer that's working well with organic traffic. Once you have an offer that converts, you can utilise paid advertising to accelerate the user acquisition process.

Ok, so fast forward a few years and you've been scaling and growing your Micro SaaS, maintaining the code base, new feature requests are drying up, it's a bit of a grind and other potential projects are catching your eye ....

Micro SaaS Shiny Object Syndrome ... it's a thing.

You might think you'd never sell your lovingly created, successful cashflowing Micro SaaS startup.

After all, this is your little baby that you've nurtured all the way from its painful birth, through the growing years that's now blossomed into a strong and independent software app.
In the next chapter, I'll be discussing reasons why you might be interested in selling your Micro SaaS app and exiting for a life changing lump sum payment.

Chapter 11

How to sell your Micro SaaS app and exit

Having grown your Micro SaaS app from nothing into a badass monthly cash generator, you might think to yourself, why on earth would I want to sell my app?!? You've worked so hard on it, you understand it intimately, and you've got more ideas on how to improve it going forward. In this chapter, I'll run through some reasons as to why you might sell your Micro SaaS app for a lump sum.

We'll then move on to the valuation and sale process as I experienced it first hand, looking at the following aspects:

- **Why Exit & Sell Your Micro SaaS app?**
- **Why I Sold My Micro SaaS Apps**
- **Valuing A Micro SaaS Business**
- **Factors Affecting The Valuation Multiplier**
- **SaaS Metrics To Constantly Monitor & Improve**
- **How I Sold My Micro SaaS Apps In 5 hours (at full asking price)**
- **From Idea To Exit**
- **What Next?**

Why Exit & Sell Your Micro SaaS?

Once you've scaled your Micro SaaS app to a certain level, the day-to-day operations may become too much for one person to handle effectively. You may need to hire a small team to help to free up your time to pull the biggest levers in your Micro SaaS business.

It's at this point that you'll want to revisit your goals and milestones that you set when you were preparing your Micro SaaS App for scaling. What targets have you hit, and what do you want to achieve from your Micro SaaS?

It's worth taking some time to consider your purpose and motivation. Do you want to work on this app for the next year, 3 years, 10 years?!? It may be that you've reached your goals, and now you've become a little less enthusiastic about the grind of ramping up your Micro SaaS. **Some days, it may actually feel like a JOB, which is what you were probably trying to escape from way back when.**

Additional Reasons You Might Sell Your Micro SaaS App:

- **Scaling Pains** - Perhaps you're better suited to developing technical solutions rather than scaling up a customer base. This could be the perfect opportunity to pass over the baton to someone with skills in organic/paid traffic.
- **Risk** - You foresee some element of risk to your apps in the near or distant future and you'd rather get out whilst the going is still relatively good.
- **Trends** - Maybe you've noticed that your niche is starting to stagnate or decline and worry about how that will affect your app's growth potential.
- **Change of scenery** - You may simply fancy working on a different technology stack or in a different niche.
- **Burnout** - Starting and scaling a Micro SaaS app isn't plain sailing. It can take a tonne of effort and you may have had enough of all the support and need to take an extended break from work.
- **Show me the money** - Simply having a life-changing lump sum paid into your bank account could just be too appealing to resist.
- **Shiny object syndrome** - You may have noticed potential opportunities in other niches and become distracted by the excitement of building something new. I am certainly guilty of this one as the image below sums up well 🤣

Why I Sold My Micro SaaS Apps

I had a crystal clear objective in my mind when I really doubled down on my Micro SaaS apps. That was simply to earn enough money from the apps to enable me to quit my unfulfilling/crappy 9-5 corporate job.

After saving up a 6 month runway and building up the monthly recurring income to be more than our family expenses, I finally jumped ship. Best. Day. Ever.

From that point on, I was motivated by fear of the apps failing and me having to go back to the corporate world with my tail between my legs.

As such, I worked tirelessly on improving the app and scaling them up to a point I felt comfortable that I would be able to survive any unforeseen circumstances (did someone say Covid-19?).

My apps made me a very comfortable living for several years and they gave me an incredible freedom that I'd never had before.

Eventually though, after the users' requests for new features quietened down and everything was running smoothly, I began to get itchy feet and noticed other opportunities for new apps in new niches. I'd spent several years working in the same niches, and whilst they were great niches, they just weren't as exciting to me as they were in the early days.

I also didn't have a huge motivation to reach the next milestones in my app growth trajectory. I figured that if the money was right, I'd sell my apps and focus on something new rather than trying to juggle too many things.

Once I'd decided that I'd be open to selling my apps, the next step was to get a valuation.

Valuing A Micro SaaS Business

At its most basic level, one of the most common formulas for valuing a SaaS business is simply:

Net Profit x Valuation Multiplier = Valuation

As a simple example, if you're making a monthly net profit of $10,000 and your valuation multiplier is x40, you're looking at a ($10k x 40) $400,000 valuation.

Note - at the risk of pointing out the obvious, several months before a sale is the perfect time to trim the fat on the business costs and to make a determined effort to boost revenue. Not only to show an upward trajectory but due to the amplification of your efforts. So, in the previous example, **if you are able to add just another $1,000 to monthly net profit that'd translate to an additional $40,000 at sale!**

There are some alternatives to the "Net Profit x Valuation Multiplier" formula. One of these is that it is common for smaller businesses (like Micro SaaS) is to use **Seller Discretionary Earnings** instead of Net Profit:

SDE = Revenue - Cost of Goods Sold - Operating Expenses - Owner compensation

Buyers like to see the true profit that's been generated by the business, rather than the amount after the founder has taken their salary/dividend payments. The **SDE** figure is then used in the valuation formula in place of net profit.

If that sounds straightforward, it's probably due to the fact that we're only dealing with financials thus far. Next, we'll look at the far more subjective factor which is the **Multiplier**.

Factors Affecting The Valuation Multiplier

1. Key SaaS Metrics

    The most important SaaS metrics you'll want to focus on improving throughout the lifetime of your apps are:
    - **Churn** - The percentage of customers that cancelled their subscriptions vs remaining subscribers in a given time period.
    - **Customer Lifetime Value (LTV)** - The average total income received from a subscriber over their subscription lifetime.
    - **Customer Acquisition Cost (CAC)** - The marketing costs needed to attract a single new paying customer.

2. Revenue Streams

    You might assume that all revenue is treated the same - money is money after all right? Well, in Micro SaaS, we have Monthly Recurring Revenue (MRR), Annual Recurring Revenue (ARR) and One Off (Lifetime) Revenue.

    You'll want to focus on driving up MRR ahead of ARR/Lifetime revenue. Whilst ARR is comforting for an owner, it's not as predictable as MRR. Also, lifetime sales are actually considered a negative to a new owner as they will need to support these customers without receiving any more income from them!

3. Profit Margin

    Simply put, the profit margin is net sales minus cost of goods sold. Clearly, the higher the margin, the better - by the nature of SaaS, it should be relatively high.

4. Age Of The Business

    A business with at least 3 years of stable performance is easier to predict, while one with less than two years of history will be more difficult. Three or more years of stable performance gives investors a much better idea of how the business will perform.

5. Niche/Market Trends

    Is the market growing or is it in decline? Do you have many competitors and if so, how does this affect your customer acquisition costs? Are these competitors fierce and are they well-funded?

6. Business Growth Trends

    Is your Micro SaaS business growing year on year, and if so, at what percentage? You might still get some interest if your Micro SaaS is trending downwards but the majority of buyers want to see a reasonable growth curve.

7. Owner Involvement & Transferability

    How involved are you with the business? Could the business run without you? The more involved you are on a day-to-day basis, the harder it is going to be to get a great multiplier for your valuation.

    - Is the code well documented (oops!)?
    - Do you have Standard Operating Procedures in place?
    - How difficult would it be to migrate the app and its assets?

8. Misc Factors

In addition to the above, there's also the following factors to consider:

- Untapped Customer Acquisition Channels
- Traffic Diversification
- Market Saturation
- Value Proposition
- Company Assets

SaaS Metrics To Constantly Monitor & Improve

As you can see, there are a large number of factors that go into a SaaS multiplier valuation that are outside of the financials!

There are some factors that you cannot directly influence, such as market trends. However, for the metrics that you can impact, you should regularly monitor your Key SaaS metrics and try to increase/decrease the following:

Increase ↑	Decrease ↓
<ul><li>Monthly Recurring Revenue (MRR) over Annual Recurring Revenue (ARR)</li><li>Lifetime Value (LTV)</li><li>Customer Satisfaction</li><li>Customer Engagement</li><li>Documentation</li><li>Operating Procedures</li><li>Your Prices (in all likelihood)</li></ul>	<ul><li>Churn</li><li>Customer Acquisition Cost (CAC)</li><li>Lifetime Sales (no matter how tempting)</li><li>Number Of Monthly Support Tickets</li><li>Support ticket response times</li><li>External Costs</li></ul>

How I Sold My Micro SaaS Apps In 5 hours (at full asking price)

After I reviewed the potential marketplaces to list my apps on, I concluded that Empire Flippers would be my preferred option. In short, whilst they primarily started off as a marketplace for E-Commerce/Amazon businesses, they had recently started to have great success with selling SaaS businesses.

When I looked into alternatives such as Flippa, they all felt a little too "Wild West" compared to the well established Empire Flippers that give great protection to both the buyer & seller with their extremely detailed vetting and migration procedures. Like everything, there are pros and cons to Empire Flippers, but for me it is the best marketplace to sell your Micro SaaS business on.

Achieving A Top 5% Valuation Multiplier For My SaaS Business

I packaged both of my chrome extensions into one listing and went through the initial Empire Flippers valuation process. This process was smooth and unlike some alternative marketplaces, the final selling price I achieved was actually very close to the initial valuation figure I received.

It's free to receive an initial valuation for your SaaS business and there's no obligation to go any further. If you're happy with the valuation range you've been given then you proceed to a final valuation. It's only at that point that you have to decide whether you'd be happy to commit to a sale if you were offered the full asking price.

The Empire Flippers vetting and final valuation process is very extensive and takes into account the factors affecting your valuation multiplier listed in the previous section. It takes a few weeks for them to verify the revenue numbers, costs, monetisation model and various data points.

This process was so detailed and extensive that I found it quite reassuring in the end. As a seller, I wouldn't want any obstacles to appear later on in the sale process (perhaps during negotiations or worse, during migration). As a buyer, I'd be very confident that the vetting team had done their job thoroughly and everything will be as advertised with no nasty surprises.

In the end, I achieved the 2nd highest ever valuation multiplier for a SaaS business on Empire Flippers, achieving a x57 monthly net profit multiplier.

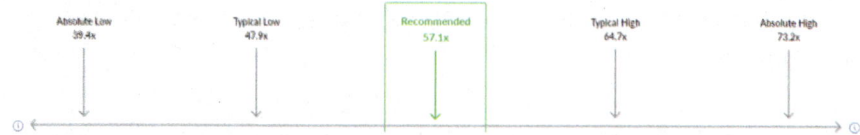

Sell Your Micro SaaS App On Empire Flippers

Empire Flippers listings go live in batches once a week on a Monday at 3pm GMT (10am ET). The normal process when these listings go live is:

1. Empire Flippers email their entire email list of active buyers.
2. Buyers unlock listing(s) they're potentially interested in (they can only unlock listings that they have proven they'd have the funds available to buy).
3. If they like what they see, Buyers arrange a call with the Seller.
4. Seller has initial calls with potential Buyers (Empire Flippers sit in on calls too)
5. Additional rounds of calls from interested Buyers.
6. Offers are submitted (price haggling is uncommon, more likely is the founder exit model)
7. Final negotiations.
8. Offer acceptance.
9. Holding deposit paid.
10. Listing made inactive on the marketplace.
11. Remainder of payment made.
12. Move to the migration phase.

However, my experience was a very much condensed version of the above as I will explain below!

Selling my Micro SaaS within 5 hours

After my listing went live in a batch on a Monday, I saw that several buyers had unlocked the listing. At this point, they'd have been reviewing the financials and the questions answered during the seller interview.

I then received a number of requests from buyers for calls. In particular, **there were a few buyers that were very interested**. They were trying to be the first buyer that I spoke with, so they'd have first mover advantage.

After a few hours, I had a few calls booked in over the next few days when something unexpected happened. One of the buyers who could only book in for the Wednesday, decided that they really wanted to buy the business and they didn't want to risk having me talk to any other buyers.

So, five hours after it went live, they bought the business at the full asking price without even jumping on a call! They paid the non-refundable holding deposit and the listing was locked on the marketplace. I couldn't believe it had sold so quickly!

Why Did It Sell So Quickly?

I believe this happened for two reasons:

1) I'd spent quite some time preparing the business for the sale which I outlined in my case study above.
2) I'd taken my time on the seller interview questions, giving as much detail as I could about the business and including potential upsides for a potential buyer.

I had a call with the buyer the next day and the rest of the sale & migration process was concluded fairly swiftly.

Final Thoughts

Selling your Micro SaaS apps can give you a life changing lump sum of cash. It is an amazingly fulfilling lifecycle to create something new, receive validation from your customer base and ultimately receive a bonus cash payment on top of the subscription payments you'd been paid til that point.

One thing that does take a little getting used to is the change in financials post-sale. Depending on whether there's an earnout or if it's a 100% cash sale then the transitions you're likely to see are:

- **Bank account**   -   Modest Savings -> Large Cash Surplus
- **Monthly income** -   Healthy Monthly Income -> Zero Monthly Income

Don't get me wrong it's a nice shift on one hand but equally it takes a little while to get your head around monthly income being reset to zero and having a lump of cash to take care of.

Finally, let's move on to the final chapter in the series, the Conclusion and Next Steps so you can find out how to accelerate your Micro SaaS journey.

Chapter 12

My Conclusions On Micro SaaS

I am a huge fan of the Micro SaaS business model. Over the past few years, it has given me such huge rewards for the time I've put into it. Specifically, through Micro SaaS I've been able to:

- **Earn** multiple 6 figures in subscription income.
- **Quit** my life-sapping 9-5 job.
- Banish **pointless meetings, office politics, chaos & firefighting.**
- Work **when** I want.
- Work **wherever** and in whatever **technologies** I want.
- Spend **more time with family**.
- Have a **better connection with the users** of the apps I develop.
- Have way more **financial stability**
- **Earn** multiple 6 figures when I finally exited and sold my Micro SaaS apps.

Let's wrap things up and dive into the following topics:

- My Journey From Idea To Exit
- What's Next For Me In Micro SaaS
- The Future Of Micro SaaS
- How To Kickstart Your Micro SaaS Journey

My Journey From Idea To Exit

My Micro SaaS journey has been quite a ride! Let me summarise it for you so you can see how I went from an unfulfilled software developer working a full time crappy 9-5 job, to quitting my job and eventually selling my apps for a life-changing amount of money.

It all started off with me simply looking to start a side hustle to bring in some more income and give me a side project that I fully owned. After I read a few self-development books, I had a lightbulb moment when I finally understood the difference between passive income vs active income.

I set out to build a side hustle that would generate passive income whilst I was at work or even better, asleep! It was also important to me that I wouldn't need to invest any money into inventory or seek funding, or anything like that to get started. I just wanted to use my spare time and my skills effectively. **That's when I discovered Micro SaaS.**

After a weekend spent hacking together my first chrome extension, I'd soon released my first Micro SaaS app. I was amazed to see that, despite being very basic and butt ugly, it was well received by the user base and even made me $3k!

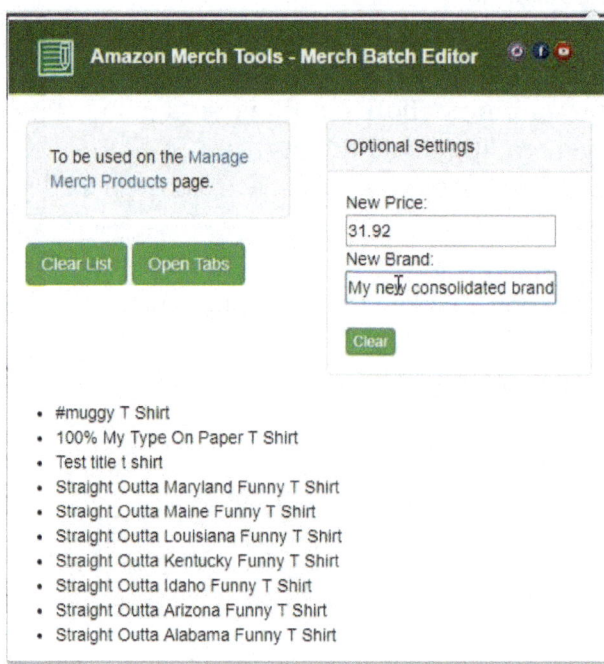

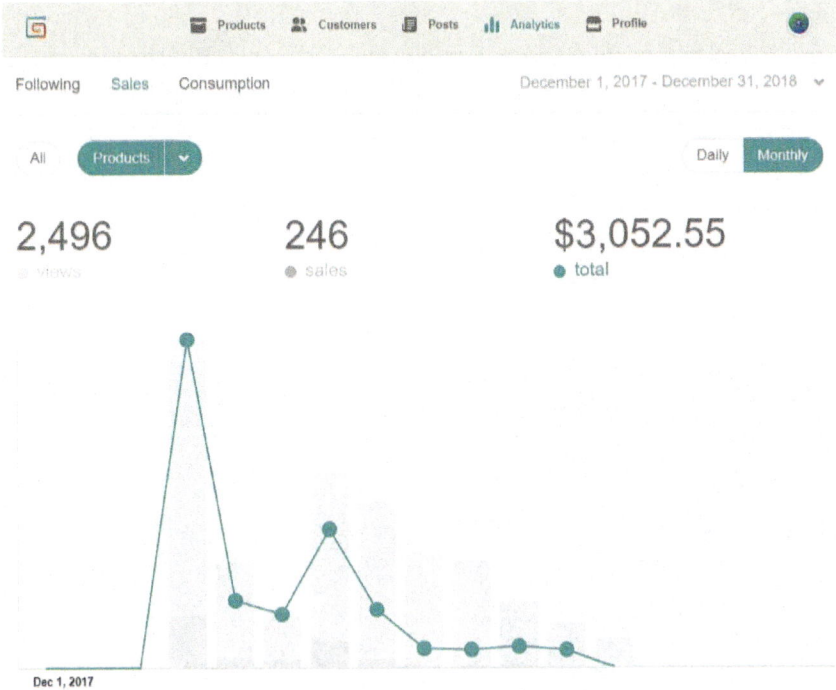

From that point on, I was addicted.

I decided to build more apps for the same niche community. One day whilst I was out walking my dog, I had an idea for a chrome extension that stopped me in my tracks (with my dog just staring at me bemused).

I felt I was on to something big and I was right. It grew into my flagship app - Merch Wizard and it changed everything for me.

I was fueled by my earlier mini app success and driven by the desire to create something bigger that could potentially lead me to quitting the day job. I could see a glimmer of light at the end of the dark tunnel and I went full steam ahead, driving for that light. **I worked tirelessly on the app during my commute, lunchtimes, evenings and weekends but it was truly a labour of love.**

Concurrently with myself working hard on developing and promoting the app, as a family we made cutbacks in order to build up a runway of savings.

After a particularly prolific Black Friday sale, I'd finally hit my runway target and the monthly subscription income was stable enough for me to finally do it .... **I QUIT MY JOB!**

No more crappy meetings/office drama/chaos/commute

More focus/family time/freedom/calm

I was able to work full time on my Merch Wizard app and scale it up. We were comfortable and enjoying the new freedoms that Micro SaaS brings. Then I launched my second app, KDP Wizard, which I managed to achieve a multi-5 figure launch with, only using organic traffic.

Fast forward a few years and my Micro SaaS apps made me multiple 6 figures in subscription income and gave me an incredible freedom that I'd never had before.

Eventually though, after the users' requests for new features quietened down and everything was running smoothly, I began to get itchy feet and noticed other opportunities for new apps in new niches. I'd spent several years working in the same niches, and whilst they were great niches, they just weren't as exciting to me as they were in the early days.

I also didn't have a huge motivation to reach the next milestones in my app growth trajectory. I figured that if the money was right, I'd sell my apps and focus on something new rather than trying to juggle too many things.

As I detailed in the how to exit your Micro SaaS app chapter, I ended up selling my apps for a very healthy lump sum payment in just 5 hours!

So, in a whirlwind ride over a few short years I had freed myself from the corporate grind and gone full circle from idea to exit. I did this using purely organic traffic, starting off with zero audience and zero ideas. I hope that this inspires you to take action because if I can do it, then so can you!

What's Next For Me In Micro SaaS

Well, in case there's any doubt, I'd like to formally announce that **I have resigned from my corporate career. It's officially over**. I'm done with the stress, crappy meetings, office politics, chaos, firefighting, trying to impress people I don't care about etc etc.

I spent 20+ years in the trenches, working my way up from Junior Software Engineer all the way up to the "pinnacle" of Technical Director, only to find it wasn't any better at "the top". Each promotion meant more responsibility which translated into more headaches and more hours.

Yes, for each promotion I was given a small salary increase, although inflation and minor lifestyle creep eroded any meaningful changes to the bank balance. It was largely a hamster wheel of pain.

Conversely, Micro SaaS feels like a deep blue ocean of opportunity with disproportionately large rewards if you get it right.

I have learnt so much on my journey, made a tonne of mistakes but I was never afraid to fail fast and fail forward.

So, firstly I want to help spread the good word of Micro SaaS and help developers to start a profitable side hustle or even to quit their full time job. I'm building up several resources to share all the knowledge I've gained up to this point.

After that, I'm going to be jumping back in the ring for Micro SaaS part two. I'm looking forward to building something bigger and better next time, utilising all the knowledge and experience I've gained. My next Micro SaaS will be built to sell from day one, bootstrapped and I'll be targeting a much bigger exit.

The Future Of Micro SaaS

I believe more and more software developers are going to discover Micro SaaS over the coming years. Many programmers will be searching for an alternative to their unrewarding corporate job.

Especially, as they'll have tasted the greater freedom and flexibility of working from home during the Coronavirus pandemic. Many software engineers have already started quitting their jobs in what's being referred to as the great resignation.

I hope that my role in all of this is to help spread the word of this different approach to earning a living. I want to show developers that they don't have to rely on being paid per hour/day/month.

Instead, for programmers to realise that there are genuine opportunities for them to utilise their existing skills in the Micro SaaS business model. This model is not constrained by the number of hours in the day and can bring in an incommensurate return on time invested.

How To Kickstart Your Micro SaaS Journey

Well done, you've finished the Micro SaaS HandBook, which has hopefully given you the high-level overview you need to go from Zero to Micro SaaS Hero.

We've gone from starting with no audience and literally no ideas, through to building a profitable bootstrapped Micro SaaS which you can sell for a lump sum if you want to.

However, this really is just a high-level overview of the basic end to end process.

If you really want to get results and stop procrastinating/over-analysing then you might want to consider applying to work with me via my coaching programme.

I've already helped several Micro SaaS founders choose their micro-niches, get lased focused on their value proposition and launch their successful MVPs and start to scale up their customer base.

If you'd like to find out more about my course & coaching programme then head over to my website at https://rickblyth.com

Cheers for now,

Rick Blyth

Printed in Great Britain
by Amazon